To my late husband, Fred "Buzz" Daigneau,
for his never-ending love and support

CONTENTS

−·−·/−−−/−·/−/·/−·/−/ ···

ACKNOWLEDGMENTS

·− ·−/− ·−·/− ·−/− ·/−−−/· −−/· −· ··/·/−· ··/−−·/−−/· ·/− ·/−/· ··

I wish to extend my sincere thanks to my editor, Jerry Pohlen, for his help and patience getting this book to completion, to former editor Lisa Reardon for her support of the project from its inception, and to Devon Freeny, developmental editor, for his help in pulling all the final details together. A huge thanks also to my agent extraordinaire, Vicki Selvaggio of Storm Literary Agency, for her guidance, support, and complete confidence as we navigate this writing road together. Special thanks to Lisa Amstutz, Mary Kary Carson, and Brandon Marie Miller, whose early encouragement and support helped push me to join them as a For Kids author.

I can't offer enough thanks to Craig Bauer, Associate Professor of Mathematics at York College of Pennsylvania, for his expert guidance and patience in helping me work through technical questions and inconsistencies. He saved me from what surely would have been many mistakes and much embarrassment! My appreciation for his help in making a sometimes technical subject kid friendly can't be expressed enough.

Thanks for the help and support of Rob Simpson, Museum Librarian at the National Cryptologic Museum, and John Brozycki, CISSP (Certified Information Systems Security Professional), for their help in answering questions and sharing some of their vast array of knowledge. A special shout-out goes to St. Patrick School (Kent, OH) teachers Jen Wohlwend and Sue O'Connor for their help guiding their students through activities included herein and to those students—Fares, Colt, Dylan, Jerzey, Kyle, Dominic, Kristina, Marianne, Aiden, Alivia, Hailey, Jace, Mason, Olivia, Holden, Annaliese, Macey, Sophia, Anthony, Maxwell, Leah, Scarlett, Patrick, Jayden, and Kevin. Their enthusiasm made it such fun for me—even those absent but there in spirit! Thanks to Josette Atkinson, Lois Cavucci, Linda Gurzenski, Debbie Hill, Cindy Idone, and Jean Kreyche—you know why. To dear friends and critique partners Gloria Adams, Joan Arbogast, LeeAnn Blankenship, Charlie Colman, Emily Levin, Judith Leisenring, and Janice Stefko—there isn't enough space here to thank you fully for your love and support on this entire writing journey. Thanks to my family—Tracy, Todd, Ty, Aaron, Eli, Christian, Ben, Rebecca, Tessa, June, Nick, Izzy, Simon, Ryan, Emily, and Lindsay—who make every day an adventure . . . in a good way! And endless thanks to my husband, Buzz, who has shared this crazy roller-coaster ride in children's publishing with unwavering support, encouragement, and love, and who never expressed one minute of doubt that this would happen.

TIME LINE

−/·· / −− / · / ·−·· / ·· / − / ·

499 BCE Histiaeus uses shaved slave's head for secret communication

487 BCE Scytale used by Greek army

196 BCE Rosetta Stone created

60-50 BCE Julius Caesar develops the Caesar cipher

9th century Frequency analysis discovered by Al-Kindi

1466–67 Leon Battista Alberti publishes first polyalphabetic cipher

1518 Johannes Trithemius publishes first printed book on cryptology, *Polygraphiae*

1586 Blaise de Vigenère publishes his first book on ciphers

1587 Mary, Queen of Scots, is beheaded for treason

1775 April 19, Revolutionary War begins

1776 September 22, Nathan Hale hanged as a spy

Summer 1778 Major Benjamin Tallmadge organizes Culper Spy Ring

1783 September 3, Revolutionary War ends

c. 1790 Thomas Jefferson creates a cipher wheel

Late 1700s France establishes the *Cabinet Noir*, or Black Chamber

1799 Rosetta Stone found

1822 Jean-François Champollion deciphers Egyptian hieroglyphics

1837 July 12, Sir Charles Wheatstone and William Cooke awarded patent for electric telegraph device

1844 May 24, Samuel Morse sends the world's first telegraphic message, from Washington, DC, to Baltimore, Maryland

1861 April 12, Civil War begins

1865 May 9, Civil War ends

1885 Beale papers published

1903 Sir Arthur Conan Doyle publishes *The Adventure of the Dancing Men*

1914 July 28, World War I begins in Europe

1917 January 16, Arthur Zimmerman sends telegram to Mexico

April 6, United States officially declares war on Germany

William Friedman begins work as a cryptanalyst for the US government

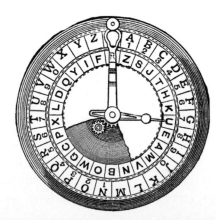

1918 Arthur Scherbius introduces Enigma machine

November 11, World War I ends

1931 November 8, Hans-Thilo Schmidt meets French agents to sell secrets about the Enigma machine

1937 Japanese Purple cipher machine created

1938 British government acquires Bletchley Park and calls it Station X

1939 September 1, Adolf Hitler invades Poland; World War I begins in Europe

December, Poland becomes the first to break the Enigma cipher

1940 September, Genevieve Grotjan finds an important pattern that helps her team complete the breaking of the Japanese Purple cipher

1940/mid-1941 Alan Turing finds keys to the German Enigma

1941 December 7, Japan attacks Pearl Harbor, Hawaii

December 8, United States officially declares war on Japan

1945 May 7, Germany surrenders to Western Allies

September 2, World War II ends with the surrender of Japan

1977 April, Ronald Rivest, Adi Shamir, and Leonard Adleman announce first public key cipher, the RSA

1988 November, James Sanborn chosen to create CIA sculpture, *Kryptos*

Early 1998 *Kryptos* messages one through three solved by CIA physicist

2001 Advanced Encryption Standard adopted by the National Institute of Standards and Technology

INTRODUCTION

··/ −·/ −/ ·−/ −−−/ −·/ ·−·/ −·−/ −/ ··/ −−−/ −·

The necessity of procuring good Intelligence is apparent & need not be further urged—all that remains for me to add, is, that you keep the whole matter as secret as possible. For upon Secrecy, Success depends in most Enterprizes of the kind, and for want of it, they are generally defeated, however well planned and promising a favourable issue.

—George Washington

· · ·

Abraham Woodhull had reasons to be concerned. As he sat at his desk on his farm in Setauket, New York, British officers—enemies of him and others in favor of breaking away from England and its king—stayed a few feet away in the room next door. Should they enter his room and catch him writing a letter to none other than George Washington, there would be no way to explain his actions. Few people, including even his family, knew of the spy activities that consumed much of his time. But Woodhull knew the consequences if he was caught. He could be imprisoned or put to death if anyone even suspected he was a spy.

Woodhull often thought of his elderly parents, who shared his home. What might happen to them if he were caught working for the Patriots? Recently, Woodhull had begun to worry that the British were aware of his frequent trips to Manhattan, supposedly to visit his sister. And that his frequent conversations with others might show a regular pattern that would arouse suspicion among British soldiers or local citizens loyal to the king.

Woodhull constantly feared being discovered. So much so that recently he had shared his concerns with Benjamin Tallmadge, George Washington's chief of intelligence. Woodhull found out a meeting had been arranged for him to meet Washington. Even though Washington knew of Woodhull's involvement in the Culper Spy Ring—Washington's group of spies—Woodhull wanted as few people as possible to know his true identity. He insisted on being referred to as Samuel Culper Sr. by anyone but close, trusted friends. British officers hardly fit that description.

Everything Woodhull did to help the growing revolution happened in secrecy. Fortunately, some actions he undertook for the cause gave him less concern than others. Searching across the waters of Long Island Sound for a black petticoat hanging on an ordinary wash line could hardly be conceived of as spy activity. But little did the British know that the sun-dried laundry gave Woodhull valuable information: Caleb Brewster, another spy for Washington, had arrived in Setauket! And who would think that four white handkerchiefs, drying in the breeze beside the petticoat, gave Brewster's exact location? He hid in cove number four.

Writing a letter to Washington, the commander in chief of the Continental Army, could hardly be passed off as leisure activity. Woodhull probably hoped that if an officer entered, he could hide the letter he was writing. His use of invisible ink added to the secrecy, which helped to alleviate Woodhull's fears. At least it was one way to hide what he was really doing.

But one thing kept him focused on his mission, even though the work was dangerous. It was the memory of the brutal death of his cousin, General Nathaniel Woodhull, at the hands of the British. That was all the reason he needed to take up the fight against them.

On this night in the spring of 1779 as he sat writing at his desk, Woodhull concentrated on the information he was sharing with Washington while listening for any sound of movement. When his door flew open, Woodhull jumped so fast his desk overturned. Papers scattered everywhere. So did the vial of invisible ink, which smashed on the floor.

Imagine Woodhull's relief—and anger—when two young girls stood before him, giggling at the joke they had played. They explained that they were only trying to shake Woodhull from his gloomy mood. Fortunately, he managed to collect enough of the spilled liquid to write again to Washington soon after. But the ink that Woodhull relied on was now almost gone—not a good situation. This new method for secret writing was one of the few things that soothed his nerves.

Woodhull and the other members of the Culper Spy Ring understood that the work they performed for the Continental Army was illegal, which made it even more dangerous. The use of codes and ciphers to spy for the cause of freedom was more important than ever.

WHAT IS CRYPTOLOGY?

The terms **code** and **cipher** are often used interchangeably. But they aren't the same. A code is a system in which a letter, number, symbol, or another word is substituted for an entire word or phrase. A cipher uses a letter, number, or symbol to replace an individual letter, combination of letters, or numbers. Sometimes, the order of the letters is rearranged.

Some codes and ciphers are so complicated that they have survived for hundreds of years and have never been broken. Some are so simple you only need a pencil and paper to **encode** or **encrypt** them, and later to **decode** or **decrypt** them.

Today there are thousands of codes and ciphers in the world, keeping us safe, making our lives easier, and helping us communicate. Some you might be familiar with, while others you may not even recognize even though you see them often. Others are used behind the scenes,

Dr. Roger Tomlin examines ancient Roman wax tablets unearthed in London in 2016. *Courtesy of and copyright © MOLA, Museum of London Archaeology*

ASSEMBLE A CRYPTOLOGIST'S KIT

Say you want to start a cryptology club. How about naming it the 4 Cs—the Code and Cipher Champs' Club?

First, you'll need to gather the right code-breaking equipment and decide where to keep your supplies. **Cryptologists,** *the name for people with jobs in cryptology, usually have to keep their work secret. They aren't allowed to talk about it, and they try not to stand out. To follow their example, you should find a good place to carry your cryptology tools that won't attract attention. An old backpack will do the trick. Do you have other ideas?*

Here are some things to gather to get started. Can you think of anything else for your Cryptologist's Kit?

YOU'LL NEED

- Pencil
- Markers
- Eraser
- Glue
- Tape
- Scissors
- Craft knife
- Small straight pin
- Assorted ziplock plastic bags or pencil case
- Small piece of paper or cardboard
- Folders (with pockets)
- Adhesive labels
- Graph paper
- Plain paper
- Notebook

- Backpack or other container for your "tools"
- Magnifying glass
- Flashlight
- Calculator
- Pocket dictionary
- Ruler and other measuring devices

1. Collect loose items such as the pencil, markers, eraser, glue, tape, scissors, craft knife, and small straight pin and arrange them in plastic bags or the pencil case. The pin can be secured by tape to a small piece of paper or cardboard.

2. Mark folders with adhesive labels— BLANK PAPER, CODES AND CIPHER TABLES, or other names—to help you organize your papers. Label another folder SOLVING DIRECTIONS AND CIPHER TOOLS to hold materials used for decoding and deciphering such as a Polybius square (see page 15). You will be adding new items to this kit as you work though the book.

3. Use the notebook to take notes or keep other information you want to record.

4. Use the backpack or other container to store all your equipment: the notebook, folders, bags/pencil case, and larger items such as the magnifying glass, flashlight, calculator, pocket dictionary, and ruler and other measuring devices.

5. Once you've gone through *Code Cracking for Kids,* you might need to reorganize your kit. You might want folders with other labels like SOLVED MESSAGES or MESSAGES RECEIVED, or whatever makes sense to you as a code and cipher champ.

so we don't even think about them or know they exist in the first place. At the heart of it all is **cryptology**—the study of codes and ciphers. And behind all those codes and ciphers are the people who make and break them.

A Lesson Learned Through Sacrifice

Nathan Hale, a spy for George Washington during the Revolutionary War, became one of the earliest casualties of the fight for independence. The 21-year-old was caught behind enemy lines, waiting to make connections for his escape, and was executed for **espionage** against the British—for spying on them. According to historical records, he had information hidden in his shoe, including sketches of British fortifications as well as notes about the British troops in the area and their positions. At that time, a formal trial was not needed to convict someone of spying. You may have heard what are believed to be Hale's last words: "I only regret that I have but one life to give for my country."

With the death of young Hale, Washington made it his mission to establish a spy network to carry out the work of those wanting independence from England. The work involved courage, patriotism, and, most important, secrecy.

Washington faced a dilemma. Say you wanted to send a note to a friend. You could write it and give it to your friend when you see him or her, but that might not be for a while. Or you could ask another friend to pass it on to him or her, or arrange to leave it on your friend's desk at school. But what if it contained a message that you didn't want anyone else to read? Maybe you're concerned it might be misplaced. What if the person

Nathan Hale was the first American executed for spying during the Revolutionary War.
US Central Intelligence Agency, courtesy of Wikimedia Commons

you asked to deliver the note decides to read it? Or what if someone sees it on your friend's desk and picks it up without your knowledge? Then your message wouldn't be a secret anymore. Someone else would have the information intended only for your friend.

By using a code or a cipher, you could make sure no one would be able to understand what your message reveals, except the one who can **decipher** it—your friend. What is the difference between your need for a secure code or cipher and

These wax tablets are from the *Novgorod Codex*, a book dating back to 1030 to 988 BCE and unearthed in July 2000 in Novgorod, Russia.
Courtesy of Wikimedia Commons

Washington's? For him it was literally a matter of life and death. One way he achieved the desired secrecy involved using a secret code.

EARLY WRITING AND WAYS TO HIDE IT

The history of cryptology and how it developed starts *long* before George Washington and his Culper Spy Ring. Since ancient times, spying and espionage have been used to win wars and dethrone rulers. In addition to other spying techniques such as double agents, secret meetings, and **dead drops**, governments around the world often used cryptology to keep information from getting into the enemy's hands. And they used **cryptanalysis** for exactly the opposite purpose: to break the codes and ciphers of their enemies and determine what they have planned.

Countries often used codes and ciphers to disguise messages. Sometimes, however, they conveyed information without encrypting it—unencrypted messages are known as **plaintext** messages—but *hid* the messages so their enemies couldn't find them. This technique is called **steganography**, which comes from the Greek word *steganos*, meaning "covered or concealed," and *graphein*, meaning "writing." The beauty of this technique was its simplicity. However, if a plaintext message was discovered, it did not take any special code skills to read it.

Most methods of steganography were simple. Others were more unusual. The Greek ruler Histiaeus would shave the head of a slave and tattoo

ANCIENT ROMAN TABLETS FOUND IN LONDON

— — — — —

In 2016, two thousand years after being used to keep accounting records, practice handwriting, and order provisions, over 400 Roman tablets were discovered at a London excavation site. They're believed to contain the world's earliest reference to London.

The wooden tablets were originally covered with blackened beeswax, and writing was pressed into the wax with a stylus. A stylus is a tool made of metal, bone, or another hard substance, with a pointed end for cutting or scratching letters and a blunt end to rub out letters and smooth the writing surface for reuse. Eventually, the wax was melted and reapplied. But after constant reuse, repeated layers of cursive writing became embedded into the wood itself.

The wood survived in the Walbrook River because it became buried in mud, which prevented exposure to oxygen. Once excavated, the tablets were kept in water until they were cleaned. Researchers treated them with a waxy substance and then freeze-dried them. Of the 405 tablets discovered, about 80 have been read. According to Dr. Roger Tomlin, a scholar of classical civilizations and an expert in cursive Latin, the process is like solving a puzzle—or like cryptanalysis.

Tomlin said he and his team photographed the tablets "varying the angles of light so as to record the whole of the scratches. Then by looking at the tablet under a microscope with a flexible light-source and using the photographs as a guide to recording what you can see, it should be possible, after a time, to start recognizing letters and even words. I should add that, like modern handwriting, you cannot read letter by letter; you have to read words, which then guarantee letters. But you start by reading individual letters. . . . Then, like a cryptanalyst, you must try out many different combinations until you find one that 'works.'"

Most interesting is information regarding more than 100 people who lived and worked in London as early as 43 CE, including slaves, freedmen, a judge, and a brewer. The handwriting sample might be evidence of the first school in London. What other secrets the tablets might reveal remains to be seen.

the message on his scalp. Of course, the slave was unable to leave to deliver the message until his hair grew back. After the slave delivered the message, a response was sometimes tattooed on his head. Again, the slave had to wait until his hair grew back before delivering the return message to Histiaeus.

Almost 2,500 years ago, the Spartan warriors of ancient Greece would send messages by covering wooden tablets with wax and then writing messages into the wax. But once, a Spartan exile living in Persia learned that the Persians were planning to invade Greece. He had to get a warning to his people without the invaders intercepting it, so he scraped the wax off a writing tablet, wrote his messages onto the wood beneath it, and then re-covered the tablet with wax. The tablet now appeared to be blank, so nobody suspected there was a message under the wax. The tablet made it to Sparta, where Queen Gorgo figured out how to uncover the message in time for the Spartans to gather their forces and meet the invaders in battle.

Herodotus, a Greek writer called the Father of History, told of a nobleman who hid a sensitive letter inside the belly of a freshly killed rabbit. His messenger set off, posing as a hunter. No one suspected that the dead animal he was carrying held a secret message.

New Ways to Solve Old Ciphers

There are two types of ciphers: **substitution ciphers** and **transposition ciphers**. They are exactly what their names imply. A substitution cipher is written by replacing the letters of a plaintext message with symbols, numbers, or other letters. With a transposition cipher, the original plaintext letters are used, but they are rearranged or shifted. A Greek **scytale** is an example of a transposition cipher.

Now try some simple ciphers. Assign each letter of the alphabet a number from one to 26 (a = 1,

b = 2, etc.). To encode the word *cipher* using substitution, replace the letters with numbers and write 3-9-16-8-5-18. You could just as easily give each letter another number, perhaps by starting with 26 and counting backward. Then the cipher would be 24-18-11-19-22-9. You could also give each letter a symbol or even make up your own designs for them. As long as the person receiving the messages has the **key**—information on what the symbols stand for—you will be able to communicate.

With a transposition cipher, you change the position of the letters but still write in plaintext. For the sentence *Meet me at the library*, you could write it backward as the single line YRARBILEHTTAEMTEEM. Or you could transpose each word individually as TEEM EM TA EHT YRARBIL. To add a twist, group the letters in a three- or two-letter pattern, such as TEE MEM TAE HTY RAR BIL or TE EM EM TA EH TY RA RB IL. These are examples of making a simple cipher more challenging.

Frequency Analysis

One advantage of a transposition cipher is that it is not subject to a method of deciphering called **frequency analysis**. It involves just what its name implies: *analyzing* the *frequency* with which certain letters appear in an encrypted message to help cryptanalysts uncover a secret message. By determining how often **ciphertext** letters, numbers, or symbols are used, and comparing those to the most commonly used letters in natural language, you can determine which plaintext letters most likely would fit into an encrypted message.

MAKE A GREEK SCYTALE

*Another unique example of steganography is a Greek scytale (pronounced SKIT-a-lee), one of the earliest military encryption methods. A strip of parchment or leather was wrapped in a spiral fashion around a baton or rod. The sender wrote the message in rows across the strip. The receiver of the message wrapped the parchment around an **identical** baton or rod to read the message. Some messengers wore the leather strip as a belt to make the message even less obvious.*

YOU'LL NEED

- 8½-by-11-inch blank sheet of paper, unlined
- Ruler
- Scissors
- Pen or pencil
- 2 additional pencils (identical in size)
- Glue or glue stick
- Transparent tape

1. Cut out two or three ½-by-11-inch strips from the sheet of paper.

2. Hold one edge of a paper strip at a slight angle on one end of one pencil.

3. Carefully wind the paper strip around the pencil, continuing at an angle, overlapping slightly to hold the paper in place.

4. For a longer message, unwind some of your paper strip and glue another strip to the end. Wind the combined strips around the pencil as in step 3.

5. When you have covered the pencil, cut off any excess paper and use a small piece of tape to hold the end in place. This tape will be removed later.

6. Write a message in a continuous row, one letter at a time, along one flat "side" or edge of the pencil. If needed, rotate the pencil slightly to continue writing your message until you are done.

7. Carefully remove the piece of tape. Unwind your paper.

8. This paper is the secret message that you share with a friend. To discover the message, have your friend rewind the paper strip on his or her own pencil, adjusting the angle of the strip as needed so the letters align.

9. To make it harder for others to read new messages, use different cylinder-shaped items for the rods, such as toilet paper, plastic wrap, or wax paper rolls; cans of vegetables or soup; or other objects. As long as you and your friend have identical items for the rods, you will be able to write and read messages.

10. Add the cylinders and scytales to your Cryptologist's Kit for future use.

This technique is effective because certain letters in certain languages tend to be used most often. For example, in the Latin or English alphabet, the letter *e* is the most frequently used letter, followed by *t*, *a*, and *o*. Less frequently used are *q*, *x*, and *z*. The most common **digraph**, or two-letter combination that makes one sound, is *th*. The Spanish alphabet contains the same letters as the English alphabet, with the addition of some accented letters. In Spanish, the most frequently used letters, in order, are *e*, *a*, and *o*. The French alphabet also uses the same letters as the English alphabet, as well as accented ones. The most frequently used letters in the French alphabet, in order, are *e*, *a*, and *s*.

In spite of the usefulness of frequency analysis, it doesn't always work. Say, for instance, you wrote a plaintext message that did not contain the letter *e*, the most frequently used letter in both English and French. This happened in 1969 when French writer Georges Perec wrote a 200-page novel without any words containing the letter *e*. If Perec had written his novel in ciphertext, imagine the challenge for cryptanalysts!

Another twist that can challenge a user of frequency analysis is a sentence such as *Will we yell wildly when we watch the Wildcats or will we wail in woe when they get walloped?* As you can see, it isn't the lack of a common letter that throws off the use of frequency analysis, but the overuse of an uncommon one.

Another way to thwart frequency analysis is to use a code instead of a cipher. Because coded symbols stand in for whole words and phrases instead of individual letters, it's impossible to crack them by looking for frequently used letters. But to communicate via code, both parties must have a codebook that shows how each word and phrase is encoded. Such books can be quite long and cumbersome compared to a cipher key.

MORE ON FREQUENCY ANALYSIS

Once you memorize some of the most common letters in any language, your codebreaking skills will automatically improve. But there are advanced techniques that can take your frequency analysis to the next level.

Besides common single letters in English, you can also look at two-letter, double-letter, or three-letter combinations. By knowing the most common examples, you'll have a better chance of cracking a cipher. The charts on the left show some of the most frequently used letter combinations in English.

Two-Letter Combinations

th	ea	of	if	in	it	is	be	as	at	so
we	he	by	or	on	do	if	me	my	up	

Double-Letter Combinations

ll	ss	ee	tt	ff	mm	oo

Three-Letter Combinations

the	est	for	and	his	ent	tha

Think about other word rules you might have learned. For example, the letter *q* is almost always followed by *u*, and *k* at the end of a word often follows a *c*. The more connections you make with frequently used and less frequently used letters and letter combinations, the better your code-breaking skills will be.

Mixing Things Up

As people became more familiar with ciphers and codes, others tried to make them more difficult to decrypt or decode. After all, what good is a secret message if the code or cipher is easy to break? One way to make a message harder to decode is by shifting the numbers assigned to the plaintext. So, where you used a *1* to stand for an *a*, you could shift the numbers you use by a given number of places. By substituting *2* for an *a*, for instance, *3* would

be *b*, *4* would be *c*, and so on up to 26, and then the number *1* would restart for letter *z*. The word *cipher* would then be ciphered as 4-10-17-9-6-19.

A substitution cipher could instead involve a different method: substituting letters for letters. If you randomly choose a cipher letter to stand for each plaintext letter, you have already added another layer of difficulty to your cipher. See the example at the bottom of the page.

Try writing a sentence substituting cipher letters for plaintext letters. When cryptanalysts do this, they typically use a lowercase letter for the plaintext and an uppercase letter for the cipher. Sometimes they do the reverse, but the format used throughout this book is plaintext in lowercase and ciphertext in uppercase. The types of ciphers that use the same ciphertext to replace plaintext throughout the entire message are called **monoalphabetic**, because *mono* means "one."

a	b	c	d	e	f	g	h	i	j	k	l	m	n	o	p	q	r	s	t	u	v	w	x	y	z
D	Y	H	L	T	P	A	X	B	Z	I	Q	G	N	V	J	U	C	O	R	K	E	W	S	M	F

USE A FREQUENCY ANALYSIS CHART

*Frequency analysis was discovered around the ninth century by an Arab scholar named Al-Kindi. It involves using sample text to determine the most frequently used letters in a given language and applying those results to an **enciphered** message. (Enciphered is another word for encrypted.) Although this tool is not foolproof, as explained elsewhere, it is still one of the foremost tools used by cryptanalysts. Today frequency analysis is mostly done by computers, but you can do a simple analysis by hand.*

YOU'LL NEED

◉ Blank or graph paper

◉ Pencil with eraser

◉ Frequency analysis chart (from step 6 of this activity)

1. On one sheet of paper, write the label CIPHERTEXT.

2. Under the label, make two rows of 26 squares.

3. Write the uppercase letters of the alphabet in the top row, in order. One letter should go in each square. The chart shown here will get you started.

Ciphertext

A	B	C	D	E	F	G	H	I	J	K															

4. Here is the encrypted message—a riddle. Rewrite it on a sheet of paper, leaving space between the rows.

VLGI   OXSUXI   EXOOGFX   BRB   ILX

OTHVEGT   VURIX?

RI'O   SHBX   HZI   LXUX!

5. Count all the *As* in the riddle and record that number under the *A* in your ciphertext chart. Then do the same for all the *Bs*, *Cs*, and so on. Here's how to start:

Ciphertext

A	B	C	D	E	F	G	H	I	J	K															
0	3	0	0																						

6. Now look at the frequency analysis chart below. The letters are in order of the most frequently used to the least frequently used in the English language.

e	t	a	o	i	n	s	h	r	d	l	c	u	m	w	f	g	y	p	b	v	k	j	x	q	z

7. Find the letter that is used the most in the riddle. Compare that to the frequency analysis chart of letters. With a pencil, write the English alphabet letter most frequently used above the enciphered letter in the riddle, *every time it appears*. For example, if *B* were the most frequent letter in the riddle, you would write the letter *e* above every *B* in the riddle. (That's not the correct answer, so don't really do that!)

8. Look at the frequency analysis chart and find which letter is the next most frequently used in plaintext. Then compare that letter with the letter that was the next most frequently used in the riddle. Substitute that letter for the ciphertext letter in the secret message by writing it above the ciphertext in the riddle. Continue substituting the next most frequent letter for the next most used letter in the riddle.

9. The frequency of a letter in the message won't always exactly match the frequency analysis chart. If a particular substitution doesn't make sense—for instance, if you end up with three vowels in a row—try moving to the next most frequent letter on the chart and seeing if it's a better fit. Don't be afraid to guess. You can always go back and erase if your guess is not right. If you skip a letter in the frequency chart, don't forget to go back and try it again with the next most frequent letter in the message.

10. If you have two letters that appeared the same number of times, think about which plaintext letter is a better fit for each ciphered letter. Do you think, for instance, that *a* might make more sense in a particular word than *o*? Again, don't be afraid to take a guess and erase it later.

11. After you have replaced two or three letters, study the message. Does it make any sense? Can you figure out any of the words? Think about common words in the English language like *the* and *it*. Continue substituting plaintext letters for ciphertext in the riddle the same way until you decipher the message. The answer can be found on page 117.

12. You can make blank frequency analysis charts and add them to your Cryptologist's Kit.

2

CODES AND CIPHERS TAKE THEIR PLACE IN HISTORY

Arab countries led the way when it came to advancing theories of cryptology and cryptanalysis. This culture pioneered advancements in medicine, mathematics, and science. In addition, literature flourished and included an interest in word games and **rebuses**, which are puzzles in which pictures or symbols replace words. It should come as no surprise that in such a creative society, secret writing also developed.

EARLY CIPHERS

The Rosetta Stone, an early cipher, was written in 196 BCE. It remained undiscovered until 1799, when Napoleon's French soldiers were rebuilding a 15th-century fort in Egypt. The fort, named Fort Julien by the French occupiers, was being expanded, and the

Hieroglyphics, like these in the temple of Isis in Aswan, Egypt, shed light on the culture of ancient civilizations.
Photo by Jorge Láscar, courtesy of the photographer

soldiers found the stone after being instructed to tear down an old wall.

The stone's name came from the small village where it was found, Rosetta (or Rashid in Arabic). The stone was originally part of a column that was approximately six feet tall. Historians believe the Rosetta Stone was moved from a temple in another location and then incorporated into the construction of the original fort.

The stone itself is approximately 45 inches tall by 28 inches wide and weighs 1,676 pounds. The granite-like rock contains writings in three different **scripts**: **hieroglyphic**, **demotic**, and Ancient Greek. The stone's messages, written by a council of Egyptian priests, included a reference to King Ptolemy V bestowing a gift of silver to the temples. In exchange, the priests decreed that both his birthday and coronation day would be celebrated annually. Parts of the original stone texts are still missing, but the surviving plaintext message helped **linguists** uncover the mysteries of hieroglyphics—an exciting development.

Dr. Thomas Young of England, foreign secretary of the Royal Society of London, learned to read at the age of two. By age 14, he had studied 12 different languages. In 1814, Young, who had an interest in Egyptology, began studying the Rosetta Stone. He made considerable progress in the study of the demotic script and the **hieroglyphs**. Though he never finished decoding the messages, he observed certain symbols surrounded by a loop, called a **cartouche**. Young correctly determined these ancient symbols must have special significance. He connected them to King Ptolemy, because *Ptolemios*, his Greek name, also appeared several times in the Greek plaintext. But Young lost interest in the project.

Fortunately, the French scholar Jean-François Champollion made a connection between the Greek plaintext and hieroglyphics. This opened a whole new world for understanding this ancient

A replica of the Rosetta Stone on display at the National Cryptologic Museum. *Photo by Buzz Daigneau, courtesy of the National Cryptologic Museum, National Security Agency*

writing system. More important, it revealed much more about Egypt and the culture of its people than previously known.

A New Way of Looking at Things

The encryption technique developed by Polybius, a Greek historian born around 200 BCE, still bears his name. Polybius's cipher, also called the Polybius checkerboard or square, consisted of a five-by-five square using the Greek alphabet. Each letter was assigned a two-number cipher, designating row first and column second, based on where it was located on the chart. For example, the cipher for the letter *s* is 43. Here is what Polybius's cipher would look like in the English language:

	1	2	3	4	5
1	a	b	c	d	e
2	f	g	h	i/j	k
3	l	m	n	o	p
4	q	r	s	t	u
5	v	w	x	y	z

Because there are only 25 possible combinations to cover the 26 letters of the alphabet, the letters *i* and *j* are combined. If you use the cipher, you can combine any two letters you want, such as *c* and *k*, or less frequently used letters like *q* and *z*. And you can arrange all the letters in the Polybius square in any order you choose. But using the

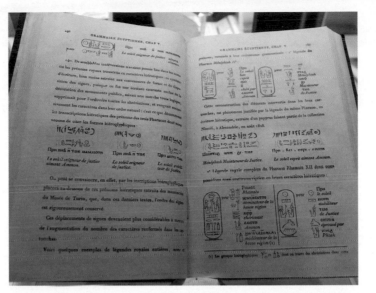

Jean-François Champollion's book on hieroglyphics, published after his death, is on display at the National Cryptologic Museum. Its complete title is *Grammaire égyptienne ou Principes généraux de l'écriture sacrée égyptienne appliqué à la présentation de la langue parlée*, which means *Egyptian Grammar or General Principles of Egyptian Sacred Writing Applied to the Presentation of the Spoken Language.*
Photo by Buzz Daigneau, courtesy of the National Cryptologic Museum, National Security Agency

HIEROGLYPHICS

- - - - -

Hieroglyphics, an ancient form of writing with pictures, dates back more than 3,000 years to Egypt. *Hieroglyphics* comes from the Greek words *hieros*, meaning "holy or sacred," and *glyphe*, meaning "carving."

Hieroglyph refers to the actual symbol that represented a letter, word, or sound. Although hieroglyphics originally referred to writing on Egyptian monuments, people commonly refer to any picture writing as hieroglyphics. The writing was first read from right to left, but later from left to right. A clue to which direction to read is the way the symbol, such as a bird or snake, is facing. The Rosetta Stone is probably the most famous example of hieroglyphics.

WRITE A MESSAGE IN HIEROGLYPHICS

Although hieroglyphics have existed since ancient times, and some of the symbols can be used to represent foreign letters, they don't match any other language perfectly. They also have symbols for syllables, which makes them even harder to decode.

   Because the hieroglyphic alphabet is not well known, and because you will add some of your own symbols to replace letters, your message should be fairly secure. Just don't show it to an Egyptian scholar!

YOU'LL NEED

- ◉ Blank sheet of paper, unlined
- ◉ Pen or pencil
- ◉ Colored pencils, markers, or crayons

1. Look at the hieroglyphs chart on the next page.

2. On a piece of paper, make two columns of boxes large enough to draw hieroglyphs inside them. Write down letters from the English alphabet that are not in the hieroglyphic alphabet, one in each box down the right column. Think of symbols for those letters. Are there ways to relate the letters to pictures? How about drawing a picture beginning with a missing letter? Will that make it easier or harder for someone to decode your message? How about thinking of an adjective instead? For instance, since a snowman is cold, you could use a snowman symbol for the letter c. Can you think of others? Draw your hieroglyph next to the letter it represents.

3. Write a message in plaintext. Then, on another sheet of paper, rewrite your message using hieroglyphics.

4. Challenge a friend to decode your hieroglyphic message. Remember he or she will need your hieroglyphic alphabet to decode the message.

5. Store your hieroglyphic alphabet chart in your Cryptologist's Kit.

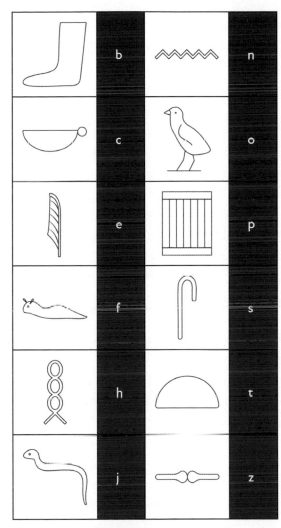

| b |
| c |
| e |
| f |
| h |
| j |

| n |
| o |
| p |
| s |
| t |
| z |

Illustrations by Lindsey Cleworth Schauer

version above, the word *cipher* would be enciphered as 13-24-35-23-15-42.

Julius Caesar had his own ciphering system. Rather than assigning a random letter or number to each letter of the alphabet, he shifted each plaintext letter by three places to produce the ciphertext equivalent—an *a*, for instance, was written as ciphertext *D*. It was one of several substitution ciphers he used as emperor of Rome from 49 BCE until 44 BCE. His most famous plaintext and ciphertext alphabets—again, in English—would look like this:

a	b	c	d	e	f	g	h	i	j	k	l	m
D	E	F	G	H	I	J	K	L	M	N	O	P

n	o	p	q	r	s	t	u	v	w	x	y	z
Q	R	S	T	U	V	W	X	Y	Z	A	B	C

This cipher may not be the hardest to crack today with the use of frequency analysis. But the fact that so many warriors at the time were illiterate would have helped keep Caesar's messages secure. While some military personnel could read and write, looking at a message like HQDFW SODQ WRQLJKW, for *enact plan tonight*, may have made them wonder if it was written in a foreign language.

When you consider all the possible shifts or rearranged combinations of plaintext letters to ciphertext letters using general monoalphabetic ciphers, the total combinations would be more than 400,000,000,000,000,000,000,000,000 individual ciphers. If you tried one possibility every second, 24 hours a day, 7 days a week, it would take you more than 12,500,000,000,000,000,000 years to try them all!

GENIUS IGNORED

From the 14th through the 16th centuries, European countries experienced a surge in classical learning, growth in business, exploration of new continents, and improvements in such things as printing and the use of paper. Leon Battista Alberti lived in Florence, Italy, in the 1460s and had many interests. Besides being a philosopher and an architect, Alberti composed and played music, painted, and wrote poetry and essays. He even produced writings on the housefly and a funeral speech for his dog!

Alberti fell into cryptology by chance when he met with Pope Paul II's personal secretary. They discussed the Pope's interest in finding a reliable cipher that would be impossible or, at the very least, difficult to crack.

While thinking about the issue, Alberti devised what some people would call the most important advancement to the world of cryptology in a thousand years: the **polyalphabetic cipher.** *Poly* means "many," and that's just what Alberti's cipher was famous for. All other ciphers at the time used just a single alphabet for an entire message. Alberti's idea, developed around 1466, added a much more challenging level to ciphering. His use of two or more alphabets to create the ciphertext for a single

message explains why he is called the Father of Western Cryptology.

In addition, Alberti invented a **cipher disk,** which allowed him to switch back and forth between alphabets when creating a message. Alberti changed the position of the disk every time a new word was written. His cipher was harder to break because frequency analysis was not helpful.

Alberti included another level of difficulty with the addition of the numbers 1 through 4. Certain important words were assigned numbers. For instance, for Pope Paul II he might use the number 167, and for the city of Rome he might use 422. This combination of a cipher and a code list is called a **nomenclator.** While Alberti was recognized for his genius in creating the polyalphabetic cipher, that didn't happen until 400 years later. At the time, people simply didn't recognize the contribution he had made to the world of cryptology.

Although Alberti's cipher was largely ignored during his lifetime, Johannes Trithemius, a German monk born in 1462, was one of the first to examine it, shortly after its creation. Trithemius had to study in secret because his stepfather made fun of his interest in learning.

Trithemius looked at Alberti's cipher and adopted the idea of a square table or tableau. The genius behind Trithemius's cipher involved using a different alphabet for *each* letter. So, in essence, 26 different alphabets—in today's English version—would be used before an alphabet repeated.

Here's how to use Trithemius's cipher, using the word *cipher* as the example. The first row of letters is the plaintext alphabet. (Although Trithemius's

Johannes Trithemius was a German monk and scholar who lived during the 16th century. *Photo by Holger Uwe Schmitt, courtesy of the photographer, via Wikimedia Commons, https://commons .wikimedia.org/wiki/File:Tilman_Riemen schneider_schuf_die_Grabplatte_des _Johannes_Trithemius_im_Neum%C3 %BCnster_W%C3%BCrzburg.jpg*

square used a row of uppercase letters across the top, this square shows the plaintext in lowercase to avoid confusion, since this book uses lowercase letters for plaintext.) For the *c*, look at the first row of ciphertext letters underneath the plaintext header, and find the one underneath the plaintext *c*. It's a ciphertext *C*, so write that down. Look at the second row. Find the letter *i* in the plaintext row at the top. Follow down the *i* column to find where the *i* column and the second row intersect. The letter *i* is replaced with *J*. For the third letter, look at the third row. Find the plaintext letter *p* in the top row and follow down the column to where it intersects with the third row. The ciphertext letter *R* replaces the *p* in your message.

Continue until you have ciphered all the letters. Here is what the word *cipher* should look like:

CJRKIW

To decipher the message, work backward, writing down each plaintext letter of the message as you go. The first letter of the enciphered message *C* remains the same. To find the plaintext letter for the second ciphertext letter *J*, look at the second row of letters, the *B* row. Move across the row to find the letter *J*, and then move up to the top plaintext row of letters. You'll see that that letter is plaintext *i*. For the third letter, you use the *C* or third row and find the letter in the enciphered message, *R*. Move up to the top row and you'll find *p*. Continue solving until the plaintext message is revealed.

Trithemius explored several different types of secret writing. One unique but simple method

Trithemius's Cipher

a	b	c	d	e	f	g	h	i	j	k	l	m	n	o	p	q	r	s	t	u	v	w	x	y	z
A	B	C	D	E	F	G	H	I	J	K	L	M	N	O	P	Q	R	S	T	U	V	W	X	Y	Z
B	C	D	E	F	G	H	I	J	K	L	M	N	O	P	Q	R	S	T	U	V	W	X	Y	Z	A
C	D	E	F	G	H	I	J	K	L	M	N	O	P	Q	R	S	T	U	V	W	X	Y	Z	A	B
D	E	F	G	H	I	J	K	L	M	N	O	P	Q	R	S	T	U	V	W	X	Y	Z	A	B	C
E	F	G	H	I	J	K	L	M	N	O	P	Q	R	S	T	U	V	W	X	Y	Z	A	B	C	D
F	G	H	I	J	K	L	M	N	O	P	Q	R	S	T	U	V	W	X	Y	Z	A	B	C	D	E
G	H	I	J	K	L	M	N	O	P	Q	R	S	T	U	V	W	X	Y	Z	A	B	C	D	E	F
H	I	J	K	L	M	N	O	P	Q	R	S	T	U	V	W	X	Y	Z	A	B	C	D	E	F	G
I	J	K	L	M	N	O	P	Q	R	S	T	U	V	W	X	Y	Z	A	B	C	D	E	F	G	H
J	K	L	M	N	O	P	Q	R	S	T	U	V	W	X	Y	Z	A	B	C	D	E	F	G	H	I
K	L	M	N	O	P	Q	R	S	T	U	V	W	X	Y	Z	A	B	C	D	E	F	G	H	I	J
L	M	N	O	P	Q	R	S	T	U	V	W	X	Y	Z	A	B	C	D	E	F	G	H	I	J	K
M	N	O	P	Q	R	S	T	U	V	W	X	Y	Z	A	B	C	D	E	F	G	H	I	J	K	L
N	O	P	Q	R	S	T	U	V	W	X	Y	Z	A	B	C	D	E	F	G	H	I	J	K	L	M
O	P	Q	R	S	T	U	V	W	X	Y	Z	A	B	C	D	E	F	G	H	I	J	K	L	M	N
P	Q	R	S	T	U	V	W	X	Y	Z	A	B	C	D	E	F	G	H	I	J	K	L	M	N	O
Q	R	S	T	U	V	W	X	Y	Z	A	B	C	D	E	F	G	H	I	J	K	L	M	N	O	P
R	S	T	U	V	W	X	Y	Z	A	B	C	D	E	F	G	H	I	J	K	L	M	N	O	P	Q
S	T	U	V	W	X	Y	Z	A	B	C	D	E	F	G	H	I	J	K	L	M	N	O	P	Q	R
T	U	V	W	X	Y	Z	A	B	C	D	E	F	G	H	I	J	K	L	M	N	O	P	Q	R	S
U	V	W	X	Y	Z	A	B	C	D	E	F	G	H	I	J	K	L	M	N	O	P	Q	R	S	T
V	W	X	Y	Z	A	B	C	D	E	F	G	H	I	J	K	L	M	N	O	P	Q	R	S	T	U
W	X	Y	Z	A	B	C	D	E	F	G	H	I	J	K	L	M	N	O	P	Q	R	S	T	U	V
X	Y	Z	A	B	C	D	E	F	G	H	I	J	K	L	M	N	O	P	Q	R	S	T	U	V	W
Y	Z	A	B	C	D	E	F	G	H	I	J	K	L	M	N	O	P	Q	R	S	T	U	V	W	X
Z	A	B	C	D	E	F	G	H	I	J	K	L	M	N	O	P	Q	R	S	T	U	V	W	X	Y

involved writing a message with **nulls**—empty spots—scattered between plaintext letters. Unfortunately, like Alberti before him, Trithemius got little recognition for his cipher.

MAKE AN ALBERTI CIPHER DISK

Different versions of Alberti's cipher disk were used through the centuries, all based on the same idea. Alberti called the larger, bottom disk the "stationary" and the smaller, top disk the "movable."

Alberti's original disk had 20 letters and four numbers. The four numbers were not used as cipher letters, so they did not appear on the movable disk. Because certain letters in the English alphabet are not used in the Italian alphabet, the disk here is somewhat different than Alberti's. For reasons that are unknown, Alberti also did not use the letters h *and* u.

ADULT SUPERVISION REQUIRED

YOU'LL NEED

◉ Copy of the two disks shown here

◉ Pen or pencil

◉ Blank paper

◉ Scissors

◉ One brass fastener

◉ Adult helper

1. Copy or trace onto a sheet of paper each of the blank disks on the next page.

2. Cut out each disk, following the lines on the *outside* of the circles.

3. Write the alphabet in lowercase around the outside of the larger stationary disk. One letter should go in each square. These are your plaintext letters. To make your cipher even more challenging, write the letters in a different order.

4. Do the same for the smaller movable disk, but write the letters in uppercase in the squares around the outside of this disk.

5. Place the smaller disk on top of the larger disk, lining up the circles closely. With the pointed end of the fastener—or

carefully with one point of the scissors (and an adult's help)—poke a small hole in the large dot in the middle of the small disk and through to the large disk. Insert the fastener, turn the disks over, and separate the two prongs until they lay flat. Your inner disk should turn easily.

6. On a sheet of paper, write a plaintext message. Pick one ciphertext letter for your starting letter. Turn the inner movable disk to line up that starting letter with the plaintext letter *a* on the outer, stationary disk.

7. Write your encrypted message on a second piece of paper. To begin with, write the enciphered letter that points to the plaintext *a*. (Remember that enciphered letters are on the inside disk and

plaintext letters are on the outside.) The starting letter is not part of the message but tells the person deciphering your message how your disks were lined up when you enciphered the first word in your message. Now write the cipher letters that are paired with the letters of the first word.

8. For the second word in your message, turn your disk again, lining up another cipher letter with the *a*. On the second piece of paper, leave a small space after the first enciphered word and then write this letter to tell where the disks line up again. Next

to it, write the second word of your message in ciphertext.

9. Continue doing this until your entire message is written in cipher. Remember, a friend deciphering your message needs to have an identical Alberti cipher disk.

10. Keep the Alberti cipher disk in your Cryptologist's Kit for future use.

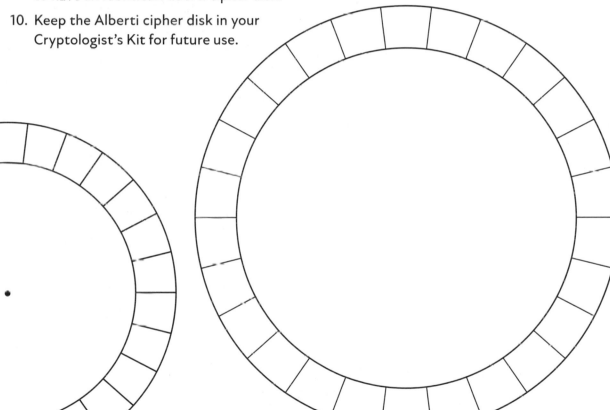

The "Unbreakable" Cipher

Remember, the harder a cipher or code is to crack, the stronger it is and the safer the secret message it hides. What if you were to use the ideas of previous cryptologists and take things even further? That is exactly what French scholar Blaise de Vigenère proposed in his 1586 book describing what many consider to be the most famous cipher ever created. Vigenère himself described it as *le chiffre indéchiffrable*—the unbreakable cipher. (Eventually, it would be broken.)

Vigenère simply took a previous idea and did a great job of describing it. People began calling it the Vigenère cipher, and the name stuck. One advantage to this cipher is that you might use the alphabet in row 3 for the first enciphered letter, the alphabet in row 23 for the second letter, and so on.

On the next page is Vigenère's cipher. Again, Vigenère used uppercase for his plaintext letters, but lowercase is used here.

Another trick to using Vigenère's method is that you could use a **keyword**, say *BURGERS*, over a plaintext message that you want to encipher. In figure 1, below left, is Vigenère's method showing a keyword along with a plaintext message.

Instead of using a different alphabet by going down row by row in order, you use the row that corresponds with each letter in the keyword. The plaintext columns and keyword rows on the Vigenère chart on the next page are marked for you—but, of course, Vigenère wouldn't have been that helpful!

To encipher the *m* from the message, you would find the *B* keyword row on the left and follow across to the *m* column. Where they intersect is the ciphertext letter *N*. For the *e* in your message, repeat those directions. Go to the keyword *U* row—the second letter from the keyword *BURGERS*—and follow across to the *e* column to get the ciphertext *Y*. Repeat these steps until you have enciphered the entire message.

It should look like this:

NYVZQVTFBZTHKZFJRXO

If you receive this message, here is how to decipher it. Again, you'll go through similar steps but work backward. Using a grid like you would to encipher the message helps. But instead of the message you want to send, fill in the second line of the grid with the message you want to decipher. It will look like the table in figure 2, to the left.

Remember, the top row is your keyword and the second row contains the letters of your enciphered message. Starting with the first ciphertext letter, *N*, locate the row that begins with the letter

Figure 1: Encipher Using Vigenère's Method

B	U	R	G	E	R	S	B	U	R	G	E	R	S	B	U	R	G	E
m	e	e	t	m	e	b	e	h	i	n	d	t	h	e	p	a	r	k

Figure 2: Decipher Using Vigenère's Method

B	U	R	G	E	R	S	B	U	R	G	E	R	S	B	U	R	G	E
N	Y	V	Z	Q	V	T	F	B	Z	T	H	K	Z	F	J	R	X	O

Plaintext

Vigenère's Cipher

Keyword Rows

	a	b	c	d	e	f	g	h	i	j	k	l	m	n	o	p	q	r	s	t	u	v	w	x	y	z
A	A	B	C	D	E	F	G	H	I	J	K	L	M	N	O	P	Q	R	S	T	U	V	W	X	Y	Z
B	B	C	D	E	F	G	H	I	J	K	L	M	N	O	P	Q	R	S	T	U	V	W	X	Y	Z	A
C	C	D	E	F	G	H	I	J	K	L	M	N	O	P	Q	R	S	T	U	V	W	X	Y	Z	A	B
D	D	E	F	G	H	I	J	K	L	M	N	O	P	Q	R	S	T	U	V	W	X	Y	Z	A	B	C
E	E	F	G	H	I	J	K	L	M	N	O	P	Q	R	S	T	U	V	W	X	Y	Z	A	B	C	D
F	F	G	H	I	J	K	L	M	N	O	P	Q	R	S	T	U	V	W	X	Y	Z	A	B	C	D	E
G	G	H	I	J	K	L	M	N	O	P	Q	R	S	T	U	V	W	X	Y	Z	A	B	C	D	E	F
H	H	I	J	K	L	M	N	O	P	Q	R	S	T	U	V	W	X	Y	Z	A	B	C	D	E	F	G
I	I	J	K	L	M	N	O	P	Q	R	S	T	U	V	W	X	Y	Z	A	B	C	D	E	F	G	H
J	J	K	L	M	N	O	P	Q	R	S	T	U	V	W	X	Y	Z	A	B	C	D	E	F	G	H	I
K	K	L	M	N	O	P	Q	R	S	T	U	V	W	X	Y	Z	A	B	C	D	E	F	G	H	I	J
L	L	M	N	O	P	Q	R	S	T	U	V	W	X	Y	Z	A	B	C	D	E	F	G	H	I	J	K
M	M	N	O	P	Q	R	S	T	U	V	W	X	Y	Z	A	B	C	D	E	F	G	H	I	J	K	L
N	N	O	P	Q	R	S	T	U	V	W	X	Y	Z	A	B	C	D	E	F	G	H	I	J	K	L	M
O	O	P	Q	R	S	T	U	V	W	X	Y	Z	A	B	C	D	E	F	G	H	I	J	K	L	M	N
P	P	Q	R	S	T	U	V	W	X	Y	Z	A	B	C	D	E	F	G	H	I	J	K	L	M	N	O
Q	Q	R	S	T	U	V	W	X	Y	Z	A	B	C	D	E	F	G	H	I	J	K	L	M	N	O	P
R	R	S	T	U	V	W	X	Y	Z	A	B	C	D	E	F	G	H	I	J	K	L	M	N	O	P	Q
S	S	T	U	V	W	X	Y	Z	A	B	C	D	E	F	G	H	I	J	K	L	M	N	O	P	Q	R
T	T	U	V	W	X	Y	Z	A	B	C	D	E	F	G	H	I	J	K	L	M	N	O	P	Q	R	S
U	U	V	W	X	Y	Z	A	B	C	D	E	F	G	H	I	J	K	L	M	N	O	P	Q	R	S	T
V	V	W	X	Y	Z	A	B	C	D	E	F	G	H	I	J	K	L	M	N	O	P	Q	R	S	T	U
W	W	X	Y	Z	A	B	C	D	E	F	G	H	I	J	K	L	M	N	O	P	Q	R	S	T	U	V
X	X	Y	Z	A	B	C	D	E	F	G	H	I	J	K	L	M	N	O	P	Q	R	S	T	U	V	W
Y	Y	Z	A	B	C	D	E	F	G	H	I	J	K	L	M	N	O	P	Q	R	S	T	U	V	W	X
Z	Z	A	B	C	D	E	F	G	H	I	J	K	L	M	N	O	P	Q	R	S	T	U	V	W	X	Y

B on Vigenère's tableau. Move across the row until you find the *N* and then move up to the plaintext row at the top. You'll see that the ciphertext letter *N* stands for *m*. For the second ciphertext letter, *Y*, you'll use the *U* row, from the keyword. Again, find the *Y* in that row and move up to the top row to see that the *Y* represents plaintext letter *e*. Continue working through the message, using the keyword rows until you have deciphered the entire message.

Mary, Queen of Scots, was beheaded for her role in attempting to overthrow the reign of her cousin, Queen Elizabeth. *Painter unknown, courtesy of Wikimedia Commons*

A QUEEN IS DOUBLE-CROSSED

Some spies and **conspirators** got so caught up in the creativity of their secret plans that they became careless and literally lost their heads. Mary, Queen of Scots, is perhaps one of the most famous examples.

Mary Stuart ascended to the throne of Scotland in 1542 CE. After a scandal surrounding her second marriage and an unpopular third marriage, the Scottish people began adopting the Protestant religion as their own. Mary, a Catholic, fled Scotland to find shelter with her cousin Queen Elizabeth I in England. But Elizabeth, afraid Mary would try to steal the throne, imprisoned her.

Mary exchanged secret messages with a Catholic supporter named Anthony Babington. Besides messages about helping Mary escape, they discussed a plot to assassinate Elizabeth. Mary and Babington used a nomenclator to communicate, with coded symbols for common words such as *and* and *with* alongside the cipher alphabet shown on the next page. However, the person who passed the messages from Mary to Babington was a **double agent**. He betrayed their trust by taking the messages to Sir Francis Walsingham, Queen Elizabeth's spymaster. When the messages were deciphered, Babington and his fellow conspirators were executed. Mary, Queen of Scots, who many supporters believed should hold the crown, was beheaded.

The conspirators' careless mistake was using the same weak cipher time and time again. Had they learned about the Vigenère cipher, written about one year earlier, Mary and her supporters might have successfully overthrown Queen Elizabeth and changed the course of history!

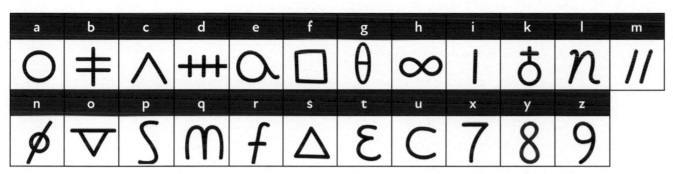

Illustrations by Lindsey Cleworth Schauer

3

COLONIES UNITED

riorto the Revolutionary War, spy activity mostly involved sneaking behind enemy lines to overhear plans being discussed and then getting back to safety without being discovered. But the Patriots realized new techniques were needed, especially following the death of Nathan Hale. More had to be done to protect Patriot spies and to increase the amount of information they could discover about the enemy—without increasing danger for the men and women involved.

INDEPENDENCE GOES UNDERGROUND

The Culper Spy Ring was established in 1778 by Major Benjamin Tallmadge under orders from George Washington. Tallmadge served as Washington's chief intelligence officer. This ring carried out day-to-day spying operations in New York City. At the time, the city was the center of command for the British forces.

When Tallmadge created the spy ring, the first person he asked to join was his childhood friend

Abraham Woodhull. But the request—and probably Woodhull's answer—came about in a most unusual way. Woodhull was a farmer who sold goods to the British Army, even though at the time the Patriots considered that activity to be unlawful. Although New York City was a British stronghold, the Continental Army controlled towns surrounding it, so the British depended on local farmers and suppliers for goods. Woodhull was one of them.

On one trip to New York to deliver goods to the British, Woodhull was caught by a Continental Navy patrol and thrown into jail. But he was unexpectedly released by the governor of Connecticut. Before Woodhull left the area, his friend Tallmadge visited him. Although the details of their meeting are unknown, it can be assumed that Tallmadge arranged his friend's release in the hopes that Woodhull would do him a favor in return—a favor not without risks. Would Woodhull join the newly formed spy ring and use his frequent trips to New York to spy on the British? The answer was yes.

What was different about Woodhull's spying techniques was that instead of sneaking into enemy camps to eavesdrop, he went about his normal activities, doing business as he always did. At the same time, he mixed with British soldiers and locals sympathetic to the king, listening for news that would aid Washington's army. From this innocent vantage point, Woodhull observed the movement of troops and learned about military plans. He even took a public loyalty oath to King George III to hide his sympathy for the Patriots.

A WOMAN PEACEKEEPER TAKES UP THE CAUSE

Among the Revolutionary War spies was a woman whose Quaker beliefs helped protect her. Lydia Darragh was living in Philadelphia when the city was captured by the British in September 1777. Although Washington attempted to recapture the city, it remained a British stronghold.

About one-third of the citizens of Philadelphia left, but because Quakers are pacifists—meaning they don't believe in supporting violence of any kind—Lydia's family felt safe staying. However, the Darraghs secretly supported the Patriot cause. Their son Charles even served in a Pennsylvania regiment.

British commander General Sir William Howe set up camp across from the Darragh home. This location allowed Lydia Darragh to spy on their activities. Eventually, the British arrived at the Darragh doorstep and demanded use of the home for meetings. Darragh convinced them to allow her family to remain.

One meeting, on December 2, 1777, was particularly important. The British made the family stay in their bedrooms after 8 o'clock. But Darragh snuck into an adjoining bedroom and hid in a closet. She overheard plans to attack Washington's army at Whitemarsh. She was concerned not only for the Patriots but also for her son, who was serving there.

Darragh's role as a homemaker allowed her to get a pass to travel across British lines to a nearby flour mill. After stopping at the mill, she walked to the Rising Sun Tavern—a favorite gathering spot for Patriot sympathizers—where she met an officer she knew. She shared information about the upcoming attack. This valuable news was relayed to Washington.

On December 4, the British attacked, but it was soon evident that Washington had been forewarned. After four days, the British returned to Philadelphia. Although they questioned Darragh, they believed her story that no one in her household was awake on the night of the fateful meeting.

Everyone Had a Job to Do

Woodhull enlisted the help of his sister and brother-in-law, Mary and Amos Underhill, who ran the Underhill Boardinghouse in New York City. The Underhills listened in on the conversations of members of the British Army staying at the boardinghouse. Then they relayed the information to Woodhull. In his first communication to Washington, Woodhull reported on the strength of the British Army and its need for more provisions. He shared information on how the Loyalists were searching local farms for livestock and other supplies. The time it took to get information from New York City to Washington's headquarters was one week—a major improvement over previous spying efforts.

In an attempt to expand the spy network, Woodhull secured the aid of Robert Townsend, who once rented a room at the Underhill Boardinghouse. Besides being a New York City merchant, Townsend owned a local coffeehouse that was popular with British officers. Townsend had numerous opportunities to rub elbows with British officers. At the same time, he overheard information useful to the Patriot cause. Townsend's alias was Samuel Culper Jr.

The success of the Culper Spy Ring advanced efforts by the Patriots to win the war of independence. In all, six members of the ring—Caleb Brewster, Austin Roe, Anna Strong, Benjamin Tallmadge, Robert Townsend, and Abraham Woodhull—operated in and around New York City for five years. None was ever discovered by the enemy. The ring was so secret that Washington himself did not know the identities of all of its members.

In spite of the ring's success, Washington remained vigilant about the need to constantly improve operations for the safety of his spies. Tallmadge used additional methods to control operating in secrecy. One of them involved invisible ink.

John Jay was another Patriot working for independence. One of the Founding Fathers, he would later become the first chief justice of the Supreme Court. His brother James was a doctor of medicine living in England who also sympathized with the Patriots. James had developed an invisible ink and, for years, the two brothers corresponded using this technique. When John Jay shared this highly classified means of communicating with Washington, the Patriot leader was extremely interested.

James Jay's recipe was different than those of invisible inks that had been used for centuries. While many ingredients—lemon juice, lime juice, milk, and other substances—revealed a message when exposed to heat, James Jay's invisible ink appeared only when a special chemical, or **reagent**, was applied. This was much more sophisticated than other methods, and one that Washington called a "sympathetic stain."

Though Washington didn't know it, the British had a similar solution and had been using it before Washington's spies. Nevertheless, the use of invisible ink eased some of the concerns of Culper Spy Ring members like Abraham Woodhull.

GEORGE WASHINGTON'S CODE

- - - - -

Another code that George Washington may have used during the Revolutionary War is provided by the National Park Service.

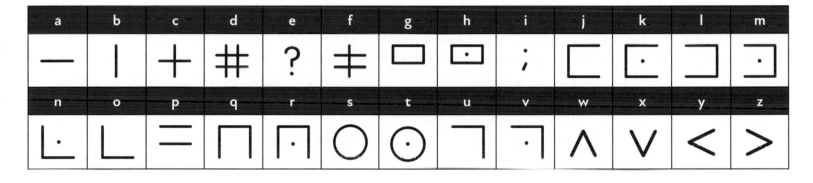

a	b	c	d	e	f	g	h	i	j	k	l	m
—	|	+	#	?	≠	▭	⊡	;	⌐	⌐·	¬	¬·

n	o	p	q	r	s	t	u	v	w	x	y	z
·⌐	L	=	⊓	⊓·	○	⊙	⌐	¬·	∧	∨	<	>

SECRETS AMONG MEN

Other Founding Fathers and Patriots used different techniques and ciphers to write in secrecy. One of these individuals was Thomas Jefferson, who would go on to become the third president of the United States.

A replica of Thomas Jefferson's cipher wheel.
Courtesy of the National Cryptologic Museum, National Security Agency

MAKE AND WRITE WITH INVISIBLE INK

The first invisible inks were juices from fruits, nuts, and plants. Today, you might experiment to see which ink works best for you and how to write with it. Writing with a toothpick or a small paintbrush takes practice too.

Keep in mind that for a long secret letter, it might make sense to write a regular letter using a pen, and then use your invisible ink to write the hidden message between the lines. Or write a fake letter, then use the back side of the paper to write your message in invisible ink. This way, anyone who captures your message won't become suspicious, because it will appear as if you are sending a regular letter!

ADULT SUPERVISION REQUIRED

YOU'LL NEED

- Cup, bowl, or other container
- Measuring cups and spoons
- Sugar
- Water
- Honey
- Baking soda
- Milk
- Lemon or lime juice
- Paintbrush or toothpicks
- Paper, preferably a "fibrous" paper, not glossy
- Several thicknesses of newspaper or a kitchen towel
- Electric iron or toaster
- Adult helper

1. Mix up a batch of invisible ink in a cup, bowl, or other container. Try these recipes one at a time. Be sure to mix well.

   Sugar-water ink: Mix ½ teaspoon sugar and ½ cup water.

   Honey-water ink: Mix ½ teaspoon honey and ½ cup water.

   Baking soda ink: Use equal parts of baking soda and water. If the mixture has clumps, try adding more water in small amounts.

   Milk ink, lemon juice ink, or lime juice ink: Use the milk or juice as is, without adding water.

2. Lay a plain piece of paper on top of several layers of newspaper or a kitchen towel. With a paintbrush or toothpick, gently write a message on the paper using one of the liquids. Do not saturate the paper.

3. Put the paper aside to dry.

4. When the message is dry, check to see if you can read it. How well is your message hidden?

5. To make the invisible ink appear, have an adult help you use an electric iron on a medium to high setting. Press it over your paper, moving it constantly so it doesn't stay over any one part of the paper for too long. Once the paper heats up, your message will appear. You can also use a toaster instead of an iron. Push down the control knob and hold the paper several inches above the toaster. **Do not** put the paper *into* the toaster.

6. Try another invisible ink. Did it work the same way? Was there an advantage to using one ink over another?

7. What other liquids can you think of to try? Some others that have been proven to work are apple juice, vinegar, and onion juice.

8. Keep your paintbrushes and toothpicks in your Cryptologist's Kit to write future messages.

KEEPING LOVE SECRET

- - - - -

One of the more interesting ways people used ciphers was to communicate with a sweetheart. During England's Victorian Era, from the late 1830s to the late 1890s, women and men were discouraged from showing signs of affection toward each other before marriage, especially in public. Personal letters that shared romantic feelings were at risk of being read first by a disapproving parent. So couples in love turned to personal columns in local newspapers to send encrypted messages to share their feelings.

Because the ciphers used were relatively simple, these so-called agony columns were open to amateur and professional cryptanalysts alike, who indulged their curiosity by deciphering messages.

Sir Charles Wheatstone, a well-known inventor in England, invented the first electric telegraph, along with William Cooke. Wheatstone also deciphered letters in London's agony columns. Apparently, he couldn't resist the temptation to respond to at least one message. An Oxford student suggested to his sweetheart that perhaps they should elope. Wheatstone wrote his own cipher message discouraging them from doing something so foolish. The woman advised her love to "Write no more. Our cipher is discovered."

MAKE A JEFFERSON CIPHER WHEEL

*When Jefferson became the US secretary of state in 1790, he realized the need for secrecy with regard to the **diplomatic** mail the United States was sending overseas. In Europe at that time, most diplomatic messages, and any letters that seemed suspicious in nature, were opened and read by postmasters. To safeguard US secrets, Jefferson invented his own cipher wheel. His design contained 36 wooden disks threaded onto a spindle. Though it's not clear whether he ever built his design—he may have instead adopted the codes and ciphers that were already in use at the time—you can create your own version with a cardboard oatmeal container and a wooden dowel.*

ADULT SUPERVISION REQUIRED

YOU'LL NEED

- Ruler with centimeter markings
- Empty cardboard oatmeal container with lid (18-ounce size)
- Scissors
- Dowel rod, 12 inches long and approximately ¼ inch in diameter
- 3 rubber bands (2 large or medium, 1 large)
- 2 blank sheets of unlined paper, cut to 6½ inches by 14 inches (you can glue sheets of 8½-by-11-inch paper end to end, then cut them to size)
- Pen or pencil
- Glue or glue stick

1. Use a ruler to measure across each end of the oatmeal container to estimate where the center point is. *Carefully* poke a small hole into each end with the scissors, approximately at the center mark. It should be large enough for your dowel rod to push through, but not turn.

2. Insert the dowel rod through one end of the oatmeal box and out the other end. The easiest way is to push the dowel rod through the bottom, take off the lid, push the dowel rod through the inside part of the lid, and then replace the lid. You might need to make your holes slightly larger.

3. Wrap a large or medium rubber band around each end of the dowel rod and push the bands close to the oatmeal box to hold the dowel in place.

4. Mark out paper strips for the ciphers. With a ruler, draw lines lengthwise on a blank sheet of paper, approximately ⅜ inch apart. You'll need to mark about 18 strips that are 14 inches long.

5. Draw 26 lines crosswise slightly less than ½ inch apart. You should have about 1 inch of unused space at the bottom of the page.

6. Before cutting the strips, write the letters of the alphabet in random order down each column. Write one letter per square. No two columns of letters should be written in *exactly* the same order, but the letters should be spaced equally apart. Cut the strips lengthwise.

7. Place one strip of paper near the lid end of your oatmeal container and wrap it

entirely around the container. Use a small dab of glue to affix one end of the strip to the other, overlapping the 1-inch space at the bottom of the strip. Make sure you do not glue the strip to the container. It should be snug enough not to move on its own, but loose enough that you can turn it.

8. Repeat step 7 for the remaining strips of paper, until you have reached the bottom end of the container. (All letters should face the same way.) The strips should not overlap.

9. Put a large rubber band around the bottom end of the oatmeal container to hold the strips in place.

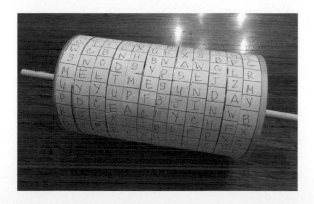

10. On a piece of paper, write a message to encipher. Beginning at one end of the cipher wheel and holding it so the letters are right side up, turn each paper "disk" until you spell out your message. If your message is too long, you can finish the rest of your message later. Use nulls (empty spaces) if your message is short.

11. Without moving any of the paper disks, slightly turn the entire cipher wheel. Choose any row and write all the cipher letters in the order in which they appear. You can use the row directly under your message or any other row. Write down the letters in the correct order. This will be the enciphered message you share with someone.

12. If you have more of your message to encipher, turn several disks in random order. Repeat step 11.

13. To decipher, a friend should line up the disks as they appear in your cipher message. Have him or her turn the wheel, again without moving any disks, until your friend finds a message that makes sense.

14. Store the cipher wheel in your Cryptologist's Kit.

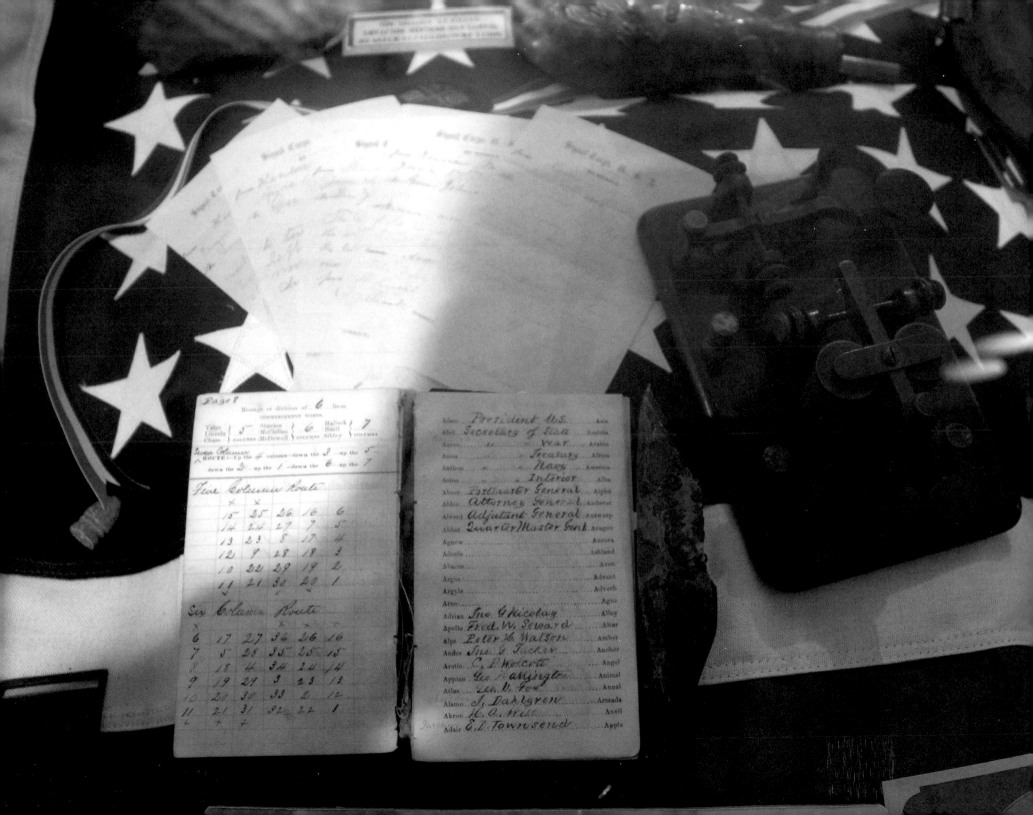

4

STATES DIVIDED

As in most other military operations, members of the Union and Confederate forces used ciphers to communicate during the Civil War. Soldiers even kept diaries and sometimes used their own systems of symbols and words to keep their personal information secret.

The Union Surges Ahead

The ciphers used by the Union Army were never cracked by the Confederates, to anyone's knowledge. But for both sides, the efforts of cryptanalysts were even more crucial than in previous conflicts, because of the role the electric telegraph played.

A Civil War Union telegraph codebook and telegraph on display at the National Cryptologic Museum.
Photo by Buzz Daigneau, courtesy of the National Cryptologic Museum, National Security Agency

An ancestor of the telephone, the telegraph allowed written messages to be transmitted quickly across long distances—a must for any army. One drawback was that telegraph messages were sent over wires, which could be tapped, allowing someone to "listen in" on other people's messages. Because it was not practical to guard every mile of wire to prevent interception, both sides enciphered their messages to prevent, or at the very least delay, interpretation.

Anson Stager, a 36-year-old telegraph operator, was put in charge of the Union's Military Telegraph Department shortly after the Civil War began. He had already created a cipher for Ohio's governor, and when asked to do the same for the Union Army, he agreed. The Stager cipher soon became the most widely used cipher during the war. Eventually, it was adopted as the War Department's official cipher.

Stager's cipher was a transposition cipher, with one difference. Called a route cipher, it involved writing the words of a message in plaintext but in columns and rows. Usually a null was added at the end of each column. Sometimes important names

(left) **A Civil War telegraph wagon like this one enabled troops to send messages from the field.** *Courtesy of the US National Archives and Records Administration, via Wikimedia Commons*

(right) **A Confederate enciphered letter written using a route cipher.** *Courtesy of the Jasper County Public Library, Special Collections*

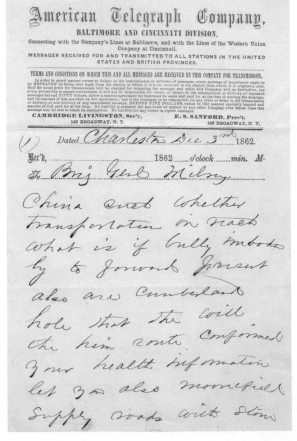

or places were substituted with code names. For instance, Stager used ADAM for Abraham Lincoln's code name and NEPTUNE to refer to Richmond, Virginia.

ROUTE CIPHERS

Route ciphers, used during the Civil War, require the message's receiver to read words in many different directions. To create a route cipher, write a message and then make a grid depending on the number of letters in your message. You can add nulls to fill in empty spaces in the grid.

To understand how it works, let's use the message "Meet at the clubhouse. Our secret is out." If you used a common down-up-down-up-down route, here is what a grid could look like:

h	b	h	t	i
m	u	o	e	s
e	l	u	r	o
e	c	s	c	u
t	e	e	e	t
a	h	o	s	g
t	t	u	r	e

After an initial null, the message runs down the first column, up the second, down the third, and so on, ending with two more nulls at the bottom of the last column. To send the enciphered message, you would write out each letter in the grid from left to right and top to bottom:

HBHTIMUOESELUROECSCUTEEETAHOSGTTURE

You could also break it into five-letter chunks of enciphered text to look like this:

HBHTI MUOES ELURO ECSCU TEEET
AHOSG TTURE

or three-lettered chunks of text like this:

HBH TIM UOE SEL URO ECS CUT EEE
TAH OSG TTU RE

Another way to write the cipher would be in a spiral pattern. Your grid would look like this:

e	e	s	u	o
s	o	o	s	h
m	u	u	i	b
e	r	t	t	u
e	s	m	e	l
t	e	c	r	c
a	t	t	h	e

And your message would look like this:

EESUOSOOSHMUUIBERTTUESMELTECRCATTHE

To decipher a route cipher, all the receiver needs to know is the layout of the grid and the direction of the route of letters.

Here are some common route cipher styles:

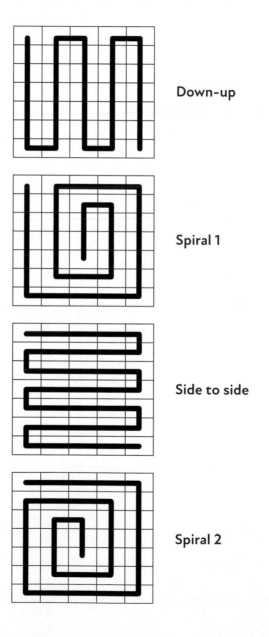

Down-up

Spiral 1

Side to side

Spiral 2

THE SOUTH FIGHTS BACK

In spite of the Union Army's success in breaking Confederate ciphers, the Confederate military officers did not stand idly by and let their messages fall into enemy hands. They, too, used techniques such as invisible ink and developed stronger ciphers to keep their plans secret.

One device the Confederates used was a Confederate cipher disk. This disk—actually two interlocking disks similar to Alberti's cipher wheel—used the Vigenère cipher system (page 22) with a keyword to encipher messages. Confederate armies often used MANCHESTER BLUFF or COMPLETE VICTORY for their keywords. Just like Vigenère, they wrote every letter of the message with a different alphabet combination.

LINCOLN TAKES AN INTEREST

One person who took a serious interest in the work of Union cryptanalysts was President Abraham Lincoln. The work of the president's cryptanalysts took place on the second floor of the War Department. Lincoln spent almost as much time there as he did in the White House, located next door, especially when battles were being fought.

Three young telegraph cipher operators—Charles A. Tinker, Albert B. Chandler, and David Homer Bates—worked closely together deciphering and enciphering a continuous flow of messages. Bates, who was only 18 years old when the war

CIVIL WAR WOMEN UNDERCOVER

— — — — —

Another Union sympathizer who participated in spy activities was Elizabeth Van Lew. She lived in Richmond, Virginia, but her Quaker schooling in the north taught her the evils of slavery. When her father died, Van Lew and her brother freed their slaves. They both spent huge sums of money to purchase and free slaves, often when a family was about to be separated.

One freed slave who previously worked for the Van Lews was Mary Bowser. Van Lew knew Confederate President Jefferson Davis's wife Varina and convinced her to hire Bowser as a servant. During her duties at the Davis house, Bowser overhead conversations about Confederate military plans that she passed on to Van Lew.

Van Lew also did a lot of charity work at Libby Prison. This involved bringing food, clothing, blankets, and other items that the Union prisoners desperately needed. But under the cover of visiting, she also carried information back and forth between the prisoners and Union officers. Sometimes she would report to the officers about the location and numbers of Confederate troops or where and when they planned to move. Van Lew also helped prisoners escape by giving them information on safe houses where they could hide. She even hid escapees in her own home.

It's been said that one of Van Lew's tricks was to pretend she was a little insane so people wouldn't think she was capable of plotting against them. Although some historians claim this is a myth, others report that people called her Crazy Bet because that's how she acted sometimes. She became so good at her work that General Ulysses S. Grant said to her, *"You have sent me the most valuable information received from Richmond during the war."*

Libby Prison, in Richmond, Virginia, was only a few blocks from Elizabeth Van Lew's mansion. She may have helped as many as 100 prisoners escape. *From Francis Newton Thorpe's book* The Civil War: The National View, *courtesy of Wikimedia Commons / Flickr's The Commons*

HIDE A CIPHERED MESSAGE INSIDE AN EGG

Elizabeth Van Lew wrote secret messages in cipher or used invisible ink. Sometimes she placed messages in the sole of a shoe, sewed them into clothing, or hid them inside a hollow egg. By tucking the hollow egg into a basket of eggs, she was able to pass along secrets to help the Union Army.

ADULT SUPERVISION REQUIRED

YOU'LL NEED

- Small pin
- Uncooked egg
- Small bowl or cup
- Pen or pencil
- Small strip of paper, no bigger than 1 by 2 inches

1. *Carefully* insert a pin into one end of the raw egg to make a pin-sized hole.

2. Turn the egg over and insert the pin into the other end. Lightly tap around the pin hole until it is about the same size as this capital O.

3. Shake the egg carefully a few times.

4. Hold the egg over the bowl with the larger hole pointing down. Gently blow into the pin hole on top until the egg white and yolk start to run out the other end. Be careful not to get any raw egg in your mouth as you blow. If you can't get the yolk and white to run out, turn the egg over and tap lightly next to the larger pin hole to make it *slightly* bigger. Continue blowing out the insides of the egg until the shell is empty.

5. Run water in a slow stream from a faucet and hold the end of the egg with the larger hole underneath the stream until the shell is about half full. Lightly hold your finger on each hole and shake several times. Then blow out the water until the shell is empty. Set the shell aside to dry and wash your hands.

6. Write an enciphered message on the small strip of paper. Roll the paper as tightly as possible, beginning with the wide end.

7. When the eggshell is dry (shake it and listen for water or blow into it to help dry it out), insert the rolled-up message into the larger hole.

8. Put the hollowed egg into a carton of normal eggs, and make your delivery just like Van Lew!

9. If you have a small box for storing your hollowed egg, you can add it to your Cryptologist's Kit.

CREATE A MESSAGE USING A DICTIONARY CIPHER

Jefferson Davis, the president of the Confederacy, communicated with one of his generals, Albert Sidney Johnston, using a dictionary code. This type of communication required Davis and the general to use the same dictionary. Dictionary code encryption involved replacing the plaintext word with a number code, such as 75-1-6. The first number indicated what page in the dictionary the word was found on, followed by the column number. The last number indicated which entry in that column corresponded to the plaintext word.

YOU'LL NEED

- Paper
- Pen or pencil
- Two identical dictionaries

1. Write a plaintext message that you want to send.

2. Look up the first word of your message in the dictionary.

3. Note the page number, column number, and entry number for that word. Write these three numbers—separated by hyphens—on your paper. (For instance, if the word is the third entry in the first column on page 250, the code would be 250-1-3.)

4. Repeat steps 2–3 for each word in your message. Each one will have a separate three-number code.

5. When your friend receives your message, he or she will be able to look up each code word by its page number, column number, and position in the column. By recording these words, your secret message is revealed!

6. Depending on the size of your dictionary, you might include it in your Cryptologist's Kit or just keep it handy to use again.

started, reported that when Lincoln first arrived each day, the president would immediately open a small drawer in one of the desks and read the recent messages recorded for him on letter-sized tissue paper. Often Lincoln stood looking over the operators' shoulders, watching letter by letter and word by word while messages were deciphered and recorded. As is true in any military operation, it was essential that the commander-in-chief knew what was happening—on the battlefield and off.

Another person connected with Lincoln also used a cipher, presumably to his advantage: John Wilkes Booth, the man who assassinated Lincoln. When Booth was killed several days after shooting the president, a Vigenère square was found in a trunk in the room he rented at the National Hotel in Washington, DC. Whether he used it to communicate with his coconspirators, or even with others involved in Confederate military operations, is not known.

THE PRESIDENT GOES INTO
THE SPYING BUSINESS

— — — — —

President Lincoln relied heavily on cryptanalysts to keep him informed. But a chance request by a publisher of Southern railroad guides may have led to one of the greatest secrets of the Civil War: Lincoln's personal spy!

A few months into the war, passports or travel passes were needed to travel north or south. According to publisher William A. Lloyd, when he approached President Lincoln for a passport to travel to Southern states to do research for his guides, Lincoln saw a perfect opportunity—a direct link to information about Confederate activity.

Lloyd claimed that he and Lincoln signed a contract, in which Lloyd agreed to compile plans about Confederate troops and activities for a $200-a-month salary. This information would supposedly be sent by courier directly to Lincoln and no one else. Ultimately, Lloyd claimed to have provided Lincoln with information on the forts of General Benjamin Huger, various maps with specific information about forts and camps, details about forts and artillery in Richmond, and the number of troops commanded by General Lee in North Carolina.

Lloyd was jailed four times during the four years he supposedly worked for the president. During one of those captures, he said, he destroyed the contract signed by Lincoln, which was hidden in his hat. Unfortunately for Lloyd, after Lincoln's assassination, Lloyd had no proof of their agreement. When he presented his bill for services to the US secretary of war, he was awarded money for his expenses—about $2,380—but was denied his claimed salary of over $9,700. Unfortunately for historians, the specific details of Lincoln and Lloyd's relationship died with each of these men. In fact, some historians believe that Lloyd was nothing more than a con man and that his entire story of spying for the president was fake!

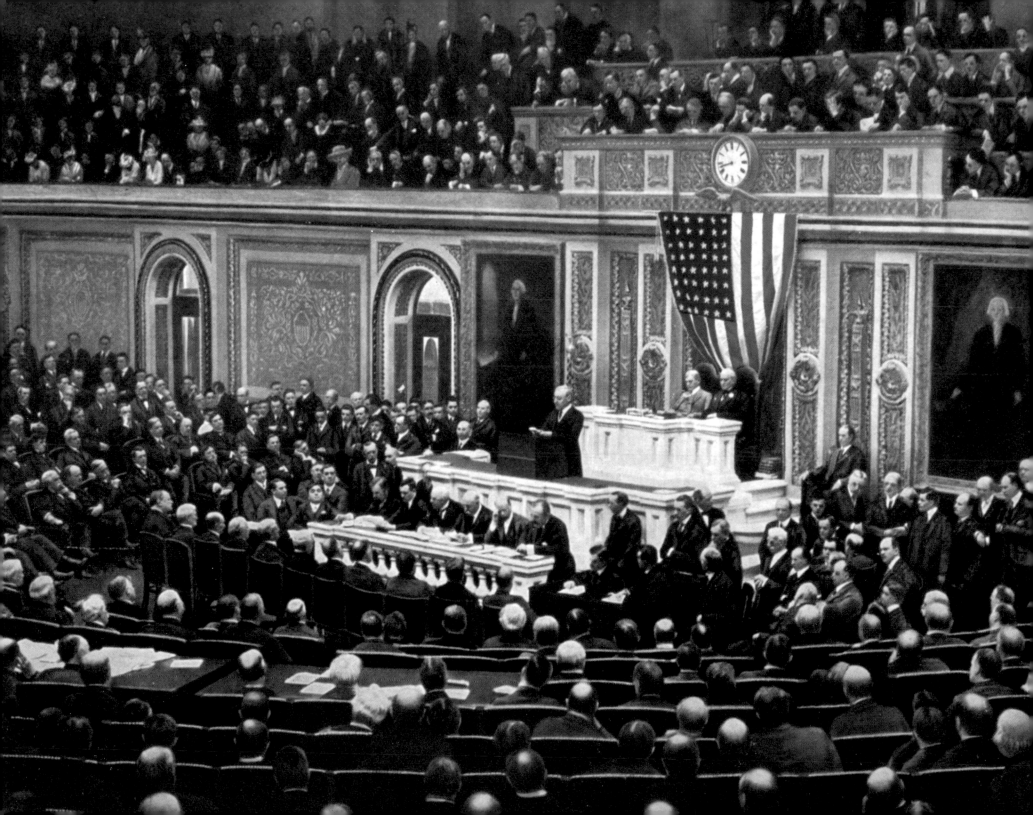

5

THE WORLD GOES TO WAR

Although codes and ciphers had been used for years in war efforts, it wasn't until the beginning of World War I that most countries established a dedicated government department to focus on foreign intelligence. Some countries, like the Allied nations of Britain and France and their major adversary Germany, had a head start on using cryptanalysts. But for the United States, a serious national crisis occurred before it recognized this crucial ingredient in staying ahead of the enemy. In fact, it was exactly that—a crisis in the form of an enciphered message—that pushed the United States into World War I in the first place.

THE UNITED STATES JOINS THE FIGHT

Before the United States joined the war in Europe, the Allies scored a major military victory over the Germans when the British cut the Germans' transatlantic cable lines. Germany

President Woodrow Wilson asking Congress to declare war on Germany. *The Library of Congress, courtesy of Wikimedia Commons*

was forced to use telegraph lines controlled by enemy forces or resort to radio communication. One advantage Germany still had was a fairly secure code and cipher system.

However, in 1914 the Russian Navy recovered a German officer's body from a sunken ship. The Russians immediately recognized the importance of the book clutched in the officer's arms—a copy of the German code. Without hesitation, they turned over the book to their British allies. British cryptanalysts were among the world's most talented and resourceful people, according to a British admiral. These men and women belonged to a dedicated department of England's intelligence forces called Room 40, named after the room in which they first worked. It wouldn't be long before the fateful discovery of this German codebook and the codebreakers of Room 40 would change the course of US history forever.

At this point, US president Woodrow Wilson saw no reason to get involved in a conflict that had no direct connection to his country's interests. But Germany was afraid that the United States would eventually enter the war on the side of the Allies. To make sure the Americans had their hands full elsewhere, the Germans attempted to encourage Mexico to take up arms against the United States. To entice the Mexican government to join forces, Germany offered money and its help in recovering land lost to the United States after the Mexican-American War. A telegram laying out the details of this plan—now known as the Zimmerman telegram—was sent from the German foreign minister, Arthur Zimmerman, to the German ambassador to the United States. The ambassador sent it on to Mexico.

But because Germany's transatlantic cables had been cut and the Germans had to use other means to send the telegram, it fell into the hands of British cryptanalysts. With help from the recovered German codebook, the codebreakers of Room 40 decoded the telegram. They immediately recognized its importance. But they faced a dilemma: How could they reveal the plaintext to the world without letting the Germans know they broke the code?

In true spy fashion, they devised their own plot. The British made it look like they'd intercepted a copy that wasn't in code. The information could be shared with President Wilson, and Germany would have no idea its code had been broken.

That attempt by Germany to involve Mexico in the war, along with German submarine attacks against passenger and merchant ships, including US fleets and passengers, turned public opinion against Germany. This pushed Wilson to abandon his previous stand. The United States joined the Allies in April 1917.

At the time, the US War Department had a separate department called the Military Intelligence Division, or MI-8. But its efforts in cryptography mostly centered around old codes and ciphers that were not very secure. Still, that didn't stop the US military and its Allied partners from doing everything possible to enable a successful end to World War I.

One of MI-8's efforts was to get its hands on other codebooks from Germany and its partners.

BUTTERFLIES AND SCOUTS

– – – – –

During the Second Boer War, which raged from 1899 to 1902, Sir Robert Baden-Powell was a lieutenant-general stationed in Dalmatia, in present-day Croatia. He used his love of the outdoors and nature to help the British effort.

With his sketchbook, butterfly net, and color box of paints, Baden-Powell wandered the countryside. If anyone approached, Baden-Powell asked if that person had seen a certain butterfly. Baden-Powell later wrote that 99 out of 100 people didn't know one butterfly from another. What he was really doing was surveying the landscape for information—information he shared with the British.

Baden-Powell knew that anyone looking at butterfly or moth drawings would have no reason to be suspicious. Little did the Boers know that hidden in Baden-Powell's sketches were drawings of military fortifications; the locations of weapons; and the layout of the local landscape, including bridges and streams.

When World War I began, Baden-Powell answered the call. At 57 years old, he volunteered to reenlist. The war secretary felt Baden-Powell's services could best be used rallying England's youth. That's because Baden-Powell had founded the Boy Scouts Association in 1907 and the Girl Guides (with his sister Agnes) in 1910.

Scouts assumed many roles during the war. When the country was bombed, they dug survivors out of the rubble. Bicycle-riding scouts blew whistles to signal the "all clear" after air raids. Sea scouts patrolled the coast, searching for mines and signs of invasion. By May of 1918, 15,000 Scouts answered a call to bring in the harvest. They guarded railway bridges, delivered war messages, and served as orderlies in hospitals.

The only British Boy Scout to die in the war was George Taylor. Taylor was 15 when he was killed in a bombing at Scarborough, a village on the North Sea.

(top) **Butterfly drawing showing a fortress and gun positions, based on the originals in Sir Robert Baden-Powell's book *My Adventures as a Spy*.** *Illustrations by Lindsey Cleworth Schauer*

(bottom) **Boy Scouts turn in plums to be weighed at a fruit farm near Cambridge, England, in 1944.** *UK Ministry of Information Photo Division, courtesy of Wikimedia Commons*

Even with plenty of work to do, the cryptanalysts' jobs would become much easier with that information. And the quicker they could decrypt messages, the quicker that information went out to the military commanders who needed it.

Finding the German codebooks became so important that the British used a diving instructor named E. C. Miller to search sunken German boats. Miller knew to look for an iron box in the officers' quarters, and he always managed to find the codebooks. Time and again, Miller found

(above) This leg from a World War II pigeon skeleton, found in a chimney in England in 2012, still had the vial to carry messages attached. *South West News Service Ltd.*

(right) The enciphered message found with the World War II pigeon skeleton. *South West News Service Ltd.*

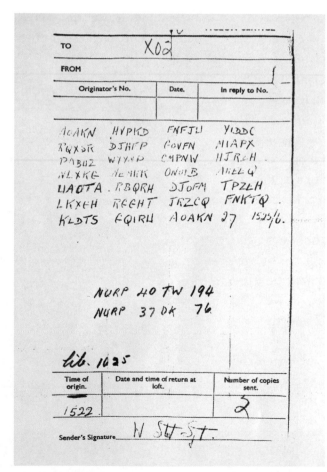

his way into the cold, still blackness, encountering seven-foot-long conger eels and dogfish that snapped at him until he threw one of his boots at the sea creatures to get away.

Cryptanalysts looked for any conceivable advantage to crack their enemy's codes and ciphers. Even the way an individual radio operator sent a ciphered message could be a source of valuable information. When an operator sent a message in Morse code—ciphered or not—he had his own way of sending it. How quickly it was sent, the length of dots and dashes, and the duration of pauses between letters and words all helped cryptanalysts identify the radio operator. This "fist" was as individual as a person's handwriting.

ANIMALS DO THEIR PART

With advances in radio technology, communication between military troops improved dramatically during World War I. But soon both sides involved in the fighting realized the need for secret codes to keep radio transmissions from being intercepted by enemy forces. Radio transmission was sometimes unreliable in the midst of battle. At other times there was a need to keep communication secret, so the enemy couldn't use radio detection equipment to determine where troops were stationed.

For those reasons, animals were pressed into service. The earliest recorded use of pigeons to send messages was 2,000 years ago by Roman military forces. Carrier (or homing) pigeons not only transferred messages quickly but also traveled to locations where difficult terrain or enemy gunfire made it impossible to string communication lines.

During World War I, there was a significant increase in the number of pigeons used for sending messages. England believed so strongly in this system of communication that it made it a crime to abuse, wound, or kill a homing pigeon. Messages were put into a vial attached to a bird's leg. Because pigeons were so fast, it was difficult to stop them from getting through to their final destinations, so there was no need to encode these messages. Only a very small percentage of these messages were written in code. These birds were so valuable that US General John Pershing successfully persuaded the US government to add a pigeon service to its Army Signal Corps in 1917. Between World War I and World War II, more than 200,000 homing or carrier pigeons were reportedly used by Allied forces.

Native Americans Step Up and Speak Out

When the United States entered World War I, only some Native Americans had citizenship status. On a national level they didn't all receive citizenship until 1924, several years after the war ended. But their strong cultural belief in defending their land and its people was one reason thousands of Native Americans from as many as 26 tribes volunteered to serve in the armed forces.

At the time, efforts were being made to force Native American children to give up their native languages and speak English. Because those native

UNLIKELY HEROES OF THE BATTLE OF VERDUN

— — — — —

In 1916 the World War I Battle of Verdun took its toll on French soldiers at the mercy of German forces. Instructed by their commanders to hold their position, the French soldiers soon were out of food and ammunition, and telephone and telegraph lines were down.

With morale at an all-time low, the troops dared to peek over their trenches. They saw nothing resembling help—until a black animal appeared out of nowhere. Recognizing it as his own dog, named Satan, a soldier named Duval urged it forward. With bullets flying, Satan seemed to fly across the scorched ground with one mission: to reach Duval.

Through the barrage of gunfire, Satan zigzagged as he had been trained. Until he was hit with a bullet. Stumbling, Satan struggled on until another bullet broke his leg. This time he fell to the ground.

Duval, determined to save his dog, climbed over the trench and urged Satan to continue. Within seconds, the soldier was dead. Somehow, Satan rose up and managed to run on three legs until he reached the French soldiers.

Satan was a sight to see. He was wearing a gas mask, and the soldiers also found a tube around his neck. It contained a message: "For God's sake, hold on. We will send troops to relieve you tomorrow." What looked like wings strapped across Satan's back were actually small baskets on both sides, each containing a carrier pigeon.

The French commander scribbled two messages giving the position of the German troops and sent them off with the pigeons. As the men watched the birds fly skyward, one was immediately shot down. But amid gunfire, the second bird escaped.

Within the hour, the sound of French reinforcements filled the air. The tide of the battle had turned. Unfortunately, Satan died of his injuries shortly after completing his mission.

LEARN THE SOUNDS OF MORSE CODE

Most people have heard of Morse code. Often they think about the person sending the message. But what about the person receiving it? While the telegraph could record a message on long strips of paper that could be deciphered later, experienced telegraph operators learned to understand the "clicks" and immediately record the letters they heard. This would be especially important during times of war.

What skills do you think you need to be able to hear and record Morse code? One way to learn this code is by saying it out loud. A tool to help you do that is a dichotomic chart or tree. **Dichotomic** *refers to something divided into two parts. For Morse code, the tree is divided into two separate sides of the chart—dots and dashes.*

A dot is actually called a dit, pronounced "dih" (short i, silent t). A dash is called a dah, pronounced exactly as it's spelled (short a, silent h). A dit was telegraphed with one quick click, and a dah was telegraphed with a longer click, equal to three dits. The space between each letter is equal to three dits, and the space between words equals seven dits.

YOU'LL NEED

- Pen or pencil
- Plain paper

← Dot/Dit   Dash/Dah →

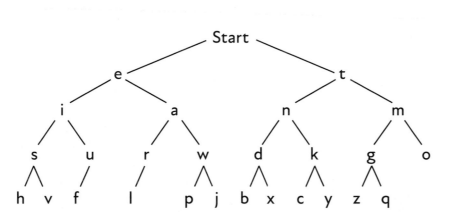

To make it easier, this tree does not include numbers or punctuation marks that are often used in Morse code.

1. Look at the dichotomic chart to the left. Thinking about frequency analysis, what do you notice about the letters? Do you see any connection with letters that are used more frequently or less frequently in the English language?

2. What else do you notice about the chart? Do you see that the dits move to the left and the dahs move to the right? This will help you learn to speak Morse code.

3. Here's how to say the letter *w*. Beginning at the word *Start*, move to the left (one dit) and say "dih" and then to the

right (two dahs) and say "dah dah" to land on the *w*. You can use your finger or a pen or pencil as a pointer to follow along.

4. Now look at the Morse code chart below. The Morse code sign for *w* is · ─ ─, which is exactly what you said earlier ("dih dah dah").

5. Write a few short words on a piece of paper. Follow the directions in step 3 for the words you've written, moving to the left for each "dih" and to the right for each "dah." Say the sounds as you move. Remember the correct pronunciation.

6. An easy way to count spaces is to tap your finger: a short tap for each dit you say and three taps as you *hold* the sound of a dah. Then pause and tap three short taps between letters and seven short taps between words. One way to practice spacing is to say any letter with dits and dahs and then tap out three beats. If you practice enough, this should become almost automatic.

7. To try this with a friend, have him or her write a message in Morse code. As dits and dahs are spoken, follow the chart and write down letters as you decode them.

8. Try longer words until you're a code champ!

Symbol	Code	Symbol	Code	Symbol	Code	Symbol	Code
a	· ─	l	· ─ · ·	w	· ─ ─	7	─ ─ · · ·
b	─ · · ·	m	─ ─	x	─ · · ─	8	─ ─ ─ · ·
c	─ · ─ ·	n	─ ·	y	─ · ─ ─	9	─ ─ ─ ─ ·
d	─ · ·	o	─ ─ ─	z	─ ─ · ·	full stop (period)	· ─ · ─ · ─
e	·	p	· ─ ─ ·	0	─ ─ ─ ─ ─	comma	─ ─ · · ─ ─
f	· · ─ ·	q	─ ─ · ─	1	· ─ ─ ─ ─	question mark	· · ─ ─ · ·
g	─ ─ ·	r	· ─ ·	2	· · ─ ─ ─	colon	─ ─ ─ · · ·
h	· · · ·	s	· · ·	3	· · · ─ ─	semicolon	─ · ─ · ─ ·
i	· ·	t	─	4	· · · · ─	hyphen	─ · · · · ─
j	· ─ ─ ─	u	· · ─	5	· · · · ·	slash	─ · · ─ ·
k	─ · ─	v	· · · ─	6	─ · · · ·	quotation mark	· ─ · · ─ ·

languages were banned in schools, they were not widely known—and so they were one of the few methods of communicating that the enemy couldn't crack. This vital solution to maintaining secrecy was discovered by accident.

At a camp of the 142nd Infantry Regiment, 36th Division, a captain overhead two Choctaw soldiers speaking in their native language. He immediately realized the advantage of having these men send and receive messages in their language and asked if there were other Choctaw soldiers engaged in the war. To confirm the idea's value, the men spoke by field telephone in their native language to other Choctaw soldiers. Their messages were translated into English. The idea was a success, and the Choctaw Telephone Squad was created.

Eventually, 19 soldiers from the 141st, 142nd, and 143rd Infantry Regiments trained for the telephone squad. Soldiers from other tribes, including Comanche, Yankton Sioux, Cherokee, Osage, and Cheyenne, eventually became involved, numbering some 400 code talkers.

The only disadvantage to using Native American languages was translating certain English military words into a language that had no such word. For instance, there is no Choctaw word for *machine gun*. So the phrase *little gun shoot fast* was used. But this disadvantage turned into an advantage: it created a code inside a code, making it even harder to break.

Random Is the Key

Near the end of the war, a new concept in cryptanalysis was developed. The US Army's cryptologic research department introduced what was called a random key. The random key consisted of hundreds of different letters listed on separate sheets of paper. As always, both the sender and the receiver needed identical copies of the key.

Using Vigenère's method, a message was sent using the first sheet of the random key. Once completed, the sender destroyed his sheet and used the second sheet for his next message. The receiver did the same after he deciphered the message. This tool became known as the one-time pad cipher, because each sheet of the pad was used only one time and then discarded.

Because the cipher letters were not repeated and the key was destroyed after a single use, other methods of solving the cipher didn't work. A cipher containing 21 letters would have about 51 quintillion different keys to test. That's 51 followed by 18 zeroes! Each sheet might look something like this:

Sheet 10

A	J	M	P	Y
M	Q	P	Z	X
H	K	O	A	Z
I	R	Z	S	H
P	E	B	T	G

And there were hundreds of them!

Unfortunately, the advantage of this system—the almost absolute security of enciphered messages—did not outweigh the disadvantages. Everyone on the same chain of communication needed to use the *exact* same key at the *exact* same time. Plus, think of the millions of alphabetic letter arrangements that would be needed—all random—when a battle raged for weeks and hundreds of messages were sent each day!

Another problem involved getting the keys—hundreds of sheets of paper—into every radio operator's hands. It was not easy when operators were scattered all over the world and engaged in battles.

The challenges of the one-time pad cipher made cryptanalysts even more determined to find something that worked, on the battlefield and off. One person who recognized the need for an organized cryptologic department was Herbert Yardley. Yardley headed the US government's MI-8 department.

Although he was unable to convince the US government to adopt the one-time pad, Yardley did convince it to set up a department solely responsible for making and breaking codes. Nicknamed the American Black Chamber, this secret organization deciphered more than 45,000 messages over a period of about 12 years.

BLACK CHAMBERS AND DARK SECRETS

- - - - -

Black chambers have existed for hundreds of years. The term *cabinet noir*—black room—was coined by King Henry IV of France in 1590. At that time, letters were sealed with melted wax and stamped, often with the seal of the sender. If the seal was broken, the person receiving the letter knew it had been opened.

King Henry had a group of talented individuals so good at resealing letters that, at first, no one knew their mail had been read by someone else. But once people began to realize their secret information was no longer secret, they started corresponding in codes and ciphers. Eventually, black chambers evolved into codebreaking centers for countries around the world.

One of the most efficient black chambers was in Vienna, Austria. Called the Geheime Kabinets-Kanzlei, or Secret Cabinet Office, it employed linguists and cryptanalysts who opened letters, copied their messages, resealed the envelopes, and returned them to the mail service. This black chamber looked at hundreds of letters each day, and most of them went through the chamber within three hours.

The staff at the Vienna black chamber weren't just interested in collecting information. They also sold this information to other European countries. They discovered secret government information about other countries and made money from it too!

Zur Beachtung!
Beachte die Gebrauchsanleitung für die Chiffriermaschine (H. Dv. g. 13).
Q W E R T Z U I O
A S D F G H J K
P Y X C V B N M L
Klappe schliessen
ENIGMA

BREAKING THE UNBREAKABLE

6

Following the end of World War I, the US Army adopted a cipher device similar to Jefferson's wheel cipher. It was surprising that Jefferson's cipher device had only recently been rediscovered at that time. But new rotor systems would soon take its place, thus changing the way countries communicated with other countries . . . and spied on them too.

Interestingly, a German inventor is credited with creating one of the hardest cipher systems to crack. And an unhappy German patriot helped the Allies crack it.

CODES AND CIPHERS GO MECHANICAL

The years following World War I showcased several advancements in cryptanalysis. One machine stands out as the granddaddy of them all—the Enigma. The most advanced

German Enigma machines, like the one pictured, produced almost unbreakable ciphers during World War II. *Shutterstock.com*

encryption and decryption machine the world had ever seen, the Enigma was developed by German inventor Arthur Scherbius in 1918. Just as Alberti's cipher changed with every letter in a message, Scherbius's device worked the same way, only better!

A simple Enigma machine worked like this: An operator typed the first letter of a plaintext message. This caused electrical impulses to travel through three rotors. A reflector on the other side sent the impulses back through the rotors, but along a different path. A bulb on the lamp board lit up showing the enciphered letter. Every time a key was pressed, a rotor would turn, sort of like an odometer on a car. Each time a rotor went all the way around, it turned the rotor next to it. But sometimes there was a position that gave an extra turn.

A three-rotor Enigma gave $26 \times 26 \times 25$ different letter arrangements before an arrangement repeated. That's 16,900 different arrangements of scrambled cipher letters before the whole thing repeated. And the rotors of the Enigma could be set manually to start at any one of those 16,900 alphabets! This made the Enigma challenging to crack.

Scherbius knew that if the Enigma machine landed in enemy hands, it would take a considerable amount of time to decrypt a message. But, ever cautious, Scherbius redesigned the rotors to make them removable, so they could be in the first, second, or third positions. A plugboard allowed yet another pair of substitutions, which took place before and after going through the rotors. The operator simply connected the letters he or she wanted swapped with a cable. Different rotor positioning combined with possible cable connections gave billions of possible encryptions.

Those billions of settings gave Germany confidence that it had found the most secure machine in the world. Germany bought tens of thousands of Enigma machines leading up to and during World War II. The Germans knew there was a slim possibility that the Enigma ciphers might be broken but believed the Allies would not be willing to put in the massive effort needed to do that.

POLAND TAKES THE LEAD

Prior to World War II, Germany had some of the best encryption in the world. But perhaps no country was more obsessed with breaking Germany's codes than Poland. The people of Poland understood that Germany wanted to regain some of the land lost to Poland after World War I. That concern forced Poland to tackle the threats head-on. For that, the country created a new cryptanalytic department, the Biuro Szyfrów—the Polish Cipher Bureau. But luck played a part too, when a frustrated German named Hans-Thilo Schmidt turned traitor. To add to the drama, it was Schmidt's older brother Rudolph who gave the official OK to use the Enigma in Germany in the first place.

After World War I, Schmidt planned to pursue a career in the army. His older brother Rudolph had been kept on and promoted, working in secret communications. The younger Schmidt expected the same, but that didn't happen. When Hans-Thilo failed as a businessman, his only choice was to ask his brother for help. That help came in the way of a position in the top-secret German department where codes and ciphers were made and broken. But living alone with his family back in their hometown, Hans-Thilo Schmidt's feelings of frustration and anger only grew. One way to get even with both his country and his brother? Sell secrets to the enemy!

When Schmidt met with an agent from France in 1931, he shared information about the Enigma machine, including instructions on how to operate it. But he did not explain how the rotors were wired inside, so that piece of the puzzle still needed to be figured out. The French weren't particularly interested in the Enigma, but they had an agreement with the Polish government to share military information, so they gave Schmidt's photographs to the Poles.

With a small group of mathematicians organized specifically to work on cracking the Enigma, the Biuro Szyfrów took on the challenge. The newly recruited cryptanalysts were from a part of Poland that had once been in German hands. With brilliant minds and the ability to speak German, they tackled the problem.

To accomplish this task took about a year of painstaking work, along with the help of Schmidt, known by his code name Asche. A machine called the bombe was created, after yet another change to the Enigma machine. The bombe was capable of finding the German key by checking all the settings in about two hours.

BOMBE

One concern was that if Germany invaded Poland—which was increasingly likely—the work of the bureau would fall into enemy hands. Before that happened, a meeting was arranged between France and England. The plan to get this information to safety involved smuggling two copies of the Enigma machine out of Poland, along with blueprints for the bombe, in the luggage of a Polish playwright. The goal was accomplished just in the nick of time. Two weeks after the machines and blueprints were smuggled out, in September 1939, Poland was invaded.

A World War II US Navy cryptanalytic bombe. *Courtesy of the National Cryptologic Museum, National Security Agency*

BLETCHLEY PARK

One of the best kept secrets of World War II was Bletchley Park. When the war started, there was concern about what would happen if London was bombed. That was where the British Army's Intelligence Unit worked. At the time Bletchley Park was called Station X or Room 40.

Bletchley Park was a privately built mansion about 50 miles from London. The first group of staffers arriving at the mansion in August 1938 pretended to be a shooting party. In reality, they were members of the United Kingdom Secret Intelligence Service's codebreaking unit and Britain's Government Code and Cipher School, which wasn't a school at all.

With radio communication, it was expected that the two million words that Germany sent in an average month in World War I would increase to two million words per *day* in World War II. The codebreakers assembled to deal with that volume of ciphered messages were puzzle fanatics, scientists, mathematicians, chess champions, and others. The test that got them through the door was solving the London *Daily Telegraph* crossword puzzle in 12 minutes or less.

As more codebreakers arrived, wooden huts appeared on the Bletchley lawn. Each hut had a specific purpose, and one hut's members had no idea what happened in most of the others. Hut 6 specialized in the Enigma ciphers used by the German Army. Once those messages were decrypted, they were passed on to Hut 3, where translation took place. Naval Enigma message decryption began in Hut 8 and transferred to Hut 4.

At its peak, about 10,000 people worked at Bletchley Park, and three-fourths of them were women. Besides breaking the Enigma, the Bletchley Park team broke the codes of Germany's Japanese and Italian allies.

Bletchley Park was where Alan Turing led the team that broke the Enigma machine. *Photo by Magnus Manske, courtesy of the photographer, via Wikimedia Commons, https://commons .wikimedia.org/wiki/File:Bletchley_Park_IMG_3625.JPG*

Britain's Room 40 took up the task of cracking the Enigma machine. The Germans were continually upgrading the Enigma to make it harder to decipher. The person who took the lead in working through the changes was Alan Turing.

Turing attacked the Enigma by using cribs—common words or phrases that could be identified in a message despite any encryption. For instance, FORT, from the German word *Fortsetzung*, meaning "continuation," was used whenever a message was a continuation of one previously sent. Sometimes simple guesswork provided a crib. Other times, old-fashioned detective work helped out. For instance, every morning at the same time the Germans radioed the weather. With a little common sense and a lot of past successes, the British determined that the message often included the word *weather*, or *Wetter* in German.

Turing's coworkers recognized his genius, even though Turing's own parents had no knowledge of what their son had done because of the secrecy surrounding this work.

RELEASE A MAN TO FIGHT

At the same time the Polish and British cryptanalysts were at work, the United States engaged in its own war on secret communication. But first the US Army and Navy were engaged in their own battle—with each other. They were fighting to recruit the best and brightest women from elite colleges and universities for an important project.

In November 1941, the navy and later the army sent out letters to thousands of young female college students. These secret letters asked two specific questions: *Are you engaged to be married?* and *Do you like crossword puzzles?* The correct answers were *no* to the first and *yes* to the second. In addition to these women, once President Franklin Roosevelt created the Women's Army Auxiliary Corps (WAAC) and, soon after, the Navy WAVES (Women Accepted for Voluntary Emergency Service), thousands of other women volunteered for duty. These volunteers played a crucial role

A Young Women's Christian Association (YWCA) poster supporting women involved in war efforts on display at the National Cryptologic Museum.
Photo by Buzz Daigneau, courtesy of the National Cryptologic Museum, National Security Agency

MAKE A ST. CYR SLIDE CIPHER

The St. Cyr slide cipher was invented by Dutch cryptologist Auguste Kerckhoffs and named for a French military academy, L'Ecole Special Militaire de Saint-Cyr. St. Cyr was a child saint who was well known in France. The academy was founded by Napoleon Bonaparte in 1803.

The school trained officers for both the infantry and the cavalry. After World War II, technicians, artillerymen, and engineers were also trained at St. Cyr, and women were admitted in 1983.

ADULT SUPERVISION REQUIRED

YOU'LL NEED

- ◉ Ruler
- ◉ Piece of thin 3-by-14-inch cardboard or poster board
- ◉ Pencil with eraser
- ◉ Old magazine or several sheets of newspaper
- ◉ Scissors or craft knife
- ◉ Adult helper
- ◉ Blank sheet of 8½-by-11-inch paper, unlined
- ◉ Glue or glue stick

1. To make the slide, measure ½ inch from each short side of the cardboard and make several marks.

2. Connect your marks on each side with a straight line.

3. Make a large dot on each line, 1 inch from the top. Do the same thing ½ inch from the bottom.

4. Lay the slide on the magazine or several thicknesses of newspaper. Using scissors or a craft knife, **carefully** poke a small hole at each dot with an adult's help. Don't cut all the way through the magazine or newspaper. (You may need to add more sheets of newspaper.)

5. Place your slide so the left edge is on top of the magazine or newspaper. Use the scissors or knife to cut through the line, between the dots. Repeat for the line on the right side.

6. Cut the sheet of paper into three 1-inch strips. Glue the strips together, overlapping the ends by about ⅛ inch.

7. Write two sets of alphabets in uppercase and in order on the sheet of paper, one after the other. Your letters should be evenly spaced about ½ inch apart. You might not use the entire strip of paper.

8. Carefully feed one end of your paper under the right side of your slide, through the cut that you made. Pull the paper across the slide to the cut on the left side and feed it through until it comes out the other end.

9. Line up the paper so that the letter A is just to the right of the cut on the left

side. One entire alphabet should show on the slide. If it doesn't, pull out the paper, erase the alphabets, and rewrite them, spacing them closer together. Reinsert the paper into the slide, again lining up the letter A with the cut on the left.

10. Write the alphabet directly above the letters on your paper, spacing them the same distance as the letters on your paper. Write in lowercase, since this is your plaintext.

11. To use your slide, move the paper and line up any letter with the *a* on the cardboard slide.

12. Write your message in plaintext, and then write the ciphertext letters, using the letters on the paper. Remember that ciphertext should be written in upper-case letters.

13. For a friend to decode your message, he or she will need to know what letter you lined up with the letter *a*. You can write this letter at the beginning of your ciphertext message as part of the first word to give your friend this information.

14. Tuck your slide cipher into your Cryptologist's Kit.

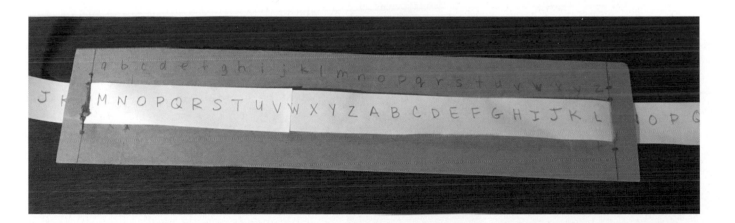

in the war effort, especially with the number of men fighting battles overseas. "Release a man to fight" became the catchphrase of the day. Women worked in factories and as chemists and air traffic controllers—anywhere men worked.

Although the ability to learn cryptography played a role in some of these women advancing to higher positions, this was not crucial. The women with the highest qualifications—often those studying science, math, and foreign languages—needed one more important qualification: unquestioned loyalty to the United States and its military efforts. Cryptography could be learned. But loyalty was a natural trait. Before a woman could be involved in this important secret work, her background was extensively checked. The smallest issue could knock a woman out of the running for a position. For instance, the US Signal Intelligence Service (SIS) required that recruits have no financial difficulties that might make them susceptible to bribery or selling secrets to the enemy.

Everyone working in cryptology took an oath of secrecy. Any breach of this oath was considered an act of treason against the government, a crime punishable by death. The women knew, of course, the work they were immediately involved in. But they didn't know how their piece of the puzzle fit into the bigger picture.

As glamorous as it might sound, the women's work was tedious, tiring, and difficult. Shifts changed regularly and, in some places, women slept 84 to a room. They all took their turns working midnight to 8:00 AM along with two other eight-hour shifts during the day and evening—all while the day-to-day activities of others took place around them.

Though the women cryptanalysts knew the seriousness of their work—men's and women's lives depended on their success—the oath of secrecy prevented them from celebrating their achievements outside work. Often, if asked what they did, the women explained that they emptied trash, made copies, or typed.

Besides breaking codes, some of these dedicated women worked to ensure US codes could

One location for World War II cryptanalysts was Arlington Hall Station in Virginia. *Courtesy of the National Cryptologic Museum, National Security Agency*

not be broken by the enemy. Some created fake messages about where US troops were or what was planned. This last technique came into play in one of the most famous battles of World War II: the D-Day invasion on the beaches of Normandy in France. Tricked by the fake messages, Germany mistakenly prepared for a battle in Norway.

By 1945 over half of the 11,000 cryptanalysts were women. But, like the Native American code talkers before them, most of their contributions have only recently been publicized and acknowledged. Many people in the 1940s believed only men could be geniuses and women were suited to more tedious work. While codebreaking could be tedious, the dedication of these women opened doors for thousands of others after them.

The Battle Moves West

Like several other countries, Germany's WWII ally Japan also began using encryption and decryption machines. The US government named one Japanese machine "Red." This was the first of many Japanese machines cryptanalysts had to contend with, which included another referred to as "Purple."

Trouble had started brewing long before this. After World War I, Japan had agreed to limit the size of its navy. All signs indicated to the United States that Japan might break that agreement. In response, the US military established listening posts to overhear Japanese communications. The US president at the time, Herbert Hoover, wanted peace and cooperation with other countries. Eventually his secretary of state, Henry Stimson, closed the American Black Chamber.

At the time, William Friedman worked for the War Department, in the Signal Intelligence Service. When the American Black Chamber closed, the SIS took over monitoring communication among other countries. But the government took a dim view of being in the spy game, and funding and staffing reached a new low.

Nevertheless, Friedman worked to build a team of cryptanalysts, and eventually his magicians, as Friedman called them, figured out the Purple's wiring system and built a replica. When Japan attacked Pearl Harbor on December 7, 1941, bringing the United States into WWII, cryptology switched into high gear. While the Purple machine enciphered diplomatic messages, the US Navy used a system called the JN-25 ("JN" for "Japanese Navy"). This code replaced words, phrases, and even syllables with five-digit strings of numbers.

But the Japanese took their encryption a step further. They took these strings of numbers and added other numbers to produce the final cipher to be sent. However, the new Japanese cipher was soon broken because the Japanese used words and phrases with patterns that cryptanalysts could guess or deduce.

In addition to their decryption efforts, the Allies continued to work on encryption methods. Their latest machine—similar to the Enigma but much better and called the **SIGABA**—had rotors that advanced almost randomly. SIGABA remained unbroken through the rest of the war.

GENEVIEVE GROTJAN

- - - - -

A high score on a math test to earn a pay raise with the Railroad Retirement Board brought Genevieve Grotjan to the attention of William Friedman, and he recruited her into the SIS. Grotjan was exactly what Friedman was looking for: her math skills, her keen power of observation, and her unending patience were perfect for the tedious task of combing through one enciphered message after another.

Around 2:00 PM on September 20, 1940, Grotjan hurried into the next room with news that she had something to share. Her boss, Frank Rowlett, knew from her enthusiasm that she was on to something. The normally quiet and reserved Grotjan would not have acted that way otherwise. Somehow, she recognized patterns in seemingly random alphabets that had been eluding her for months. This recognition was the breakthrough needed to crack Japan's Purple cipher. The group of cryptanalysts took a break, sent out for Cokes, and then went back to work.

At the time of her discovery, the United States was not at war with Japan, although tensions were mounting. Grotjan's work enabled the team to build a model Purple machine that one admiral said literally shortened the length of the war. Years later in an interview, Grotjan modestly said, "Maybe I was just lucky."

Her husband, Hyman I. Feinstein, also worked on secret projects for the government. During the course of their marriage, Grotjan Feinstein, as she was sometimes referred to after her marriage, shared that they knew little about the work the other was doing because of its top-secret nature. Feinstein established the Genevieve Feinstein Award in Cryptography at George Mason University, which is still awarded today to exceptional mathematics undergraduates. Grotjan Feinstein established a scholarship in the name of her deceased son Ellis, her only child. She was inducted into the National Security Agency (NSA) Cryptologic Hall of Honor in 2011, five years after her death at age 93.

NATIVE AMERICANS STEP UP AGAIN

Just as they did in World War I, Native Americans supported the war efforts in World War II. Their involvement as code talkers had a similar origin as in World War I. Philip Johnston, an engineer who wanted to enlist but was past the age limit, decided to use his childhood experiences growing up among the Navajo to create a communication system that would almost guarantee secrecy.

Johnston approached a signal officer about using the Navajo language as a military code. As before, a trial run was conducted involving two Navajo natives who were separated but communicated successfully by radio. The only difference this time was that a number of Germans actually spoke and understood some Native American languages. In addition, the same language issue that occurred in World War I arose again—how to use Native American languages to speak about concepts that were not part of Native American culture. And lastly, there needed to be enough men to fill all the positions necessary.

The largest Native American tribes at the time were the Sioux, the Chippewa, the Pima-Papago, and the Navajo. While Navajo people had less formal education than people from other tribes, their culture was less studied by the Germans. In addition to that advantage, the Navajo language is totally different than any other tribal language. Even other Native Americans would have trouble understanding Navajo messages.

As for the recurring language issue, the US military commanders again devised a code within a code. Some military words were assigned Navajo words, such as *Lo-tso* (whale) for battleship, *Beshi-lo* (iron fish) for submarine, and *A-ye-shi* (eggs) for bombs.

Also created was a lexicon—an alphabetical arrangement of letters—using the Navajo language. When an operator needed to give a specific geographic location or the name of a commander, the code talkers would spell out the English word in the Navajo alphabet.

But increased use of the lexicon also provoked concerns. First of all, spelling out words took extra time, which was scarce in the middle of a battle. And second, it meant the messages were vulnerable to frequency analysis. If the enemy noticed the repeated use of a common letter like *dzeh*—or *e* for *elk*—the message could be decrypted.

To address these problems, another 234 terms were added to the code so fewer words would need to be spelled out. And to thwart frequency analysis on the remaining spelled-out terms, the lexicon was updated so that multiple words could replace common letters. Three different words stood for the most common letters, with two for the next most common letters.

Here's a sampling of the expanded Navajo code talkers' lexicon from June 1945:

A	Ant	Wol-la-chee
A	Apple	Be-la-sana
A	Axe	Tse-nill
E	Ear	Ah-jah
E	Elk	Dzeh
E	Eye	Ah-nah
K	Kid	Klizzie-yazzie
L	Lamb	Dibeh-yazzie
L	Leg	Ah-jad
N	Needle	Tsah
N	Noise	Ah-chin
N	Nut	Nesh-chee
T	Tea	D-ah
T	Tooth	A-woh
T	Turkey	Than-zie
V	Victor	A-keh-di-glini
Y	Yuca	Tash-as-zih
Z	Zinc	Besh-do-tliz

Thus, to encode the word *navy*, a code talker could say either "Tsah-wol-la-chee-a-keh-di-glini-tash-as-zih" or "Ah-chin-be-la-sana-a-keh-di-glini-tash-as-zih," or several other combinations of letters. Imagine the difficulty decoding a word that used even more common letters, such as *troops*. The code was never broken.

Despite the contribution the Navajo code talkers made to winning the war, they weren't allowed to talk about their work—at least not until 1968, when the information was **declassified** and their true contributions became known.

70 Years Later: World War II Coded Letters Revealed

British sublieutenant John Pryor diligently wrote 20 letters to his family during the five years he was a prisoner of war (POW) in Germany. Pryor talked about such everyday subjects as gardening, sailing books, and items like chocolate and cigarettes. But before his family read them, the letters were deciphered by the cryptanalysts of MI9, a department of the British War Office. The letters revealed important information about German ammunition stockpiles and military strategies.

The code used by Pryor and others was so complicated that 70 years later, when the letters were shared by his grandson Stephen with historians at the University of Plymouth in England, they failed to decipher them. Ultimately, mathematician David McMullan discovered the key by examining certain words whose initial letters revealed a grid that revealed yet more letters and numbers.

A POW escape committee gave prisoners the information to be included in their letters. Prisoners were allowed to send letters home as a special privilege, such as for good behavior. But first they were examined by German censors and then British codebreakers.

In one letter Pryor wrote, "Many seeds are left being saved from several plants, which did very well some time ago. Our last year's harvest was extremely good. Well worth repeating again for this year." What he was actually reporting on was the failure of a German submarine attack in 1940. Besides information about military plans, prisoners requested items like maps and currency to help them escape. The way the POWs dated their letters, using a "3/26/41" format instead of "March 26, 1941" and underlining their signatures, gave a clear indication that the letter contained coded information.

Pryor later wrote about his life but was unable to remember the key for the code, and he died without ever telling his family about it.

Long May They Wave

Another communication method used by military forces in World War II is still in use today: the navy signal flag system. People have utilized flags or similar objects to signal across long distances since as far back as 200 BCE. One of the earliest refined systems was developed in 1694 by Charles Hooke in England, but its use remained limited.

LEARN TO USE THE VIETNAM PRISONER OF WAR TAP CODE

The tap code used by POWs in the Vietnam War was actually first used in World War II. It remained an effective and safe way for prisoners to communicate secretly. Since the tap code was never written down, it remained hidden from the enemy, an important benefit for those who used it. In addition, it could easily be taught to new arrivals.

As is true for many codes and ciphers, it was not unusual to use an abbreviated version to make communicating easier and faster. For instance, according to Retired Navy Captain Gerald L. "Jerry" Coffee, GN stood for "Good night," while GBU stood for "God bless you." Coffee said the message "Good night. God bless America" was tapped as a way of signing off "every single night." Communicating this way not only helped prisoners know what was going on but also helped boost morale when things got especially difficult.

YOU'LL NEED

◉ The tap code key below

	1	2	3	4	5
1	A	B	C/K	D	E
2	F	G	H	I	J
3	L	M	N	O	P
4	Q	R	S	T	U
5	V	W	X	Y	Z

1. With the tap code, the number of the column is tapped first, followed by a pause, and then the number of the row.

2. For the letter *r*, you would tap two times, then pause and tap four times. Letter *a* is tapped once, followed by a pause and then one more tap. You can see from the chart that *c* and *k* share the same number of taps, because they also share the same sounds.

3. You can tap on a table, a book, or just about anywhere, using your finger. As long as others can hear your taps, your message can be understood.

4. Can you make up other shortcut words that you can tap and share with a friend?

VIETNAM VETERAN BLINKED *TORTURE* IN MORSE CODE

– – – – –

US Navy officer Jeremiah Denton was held captive by North Vietnam for more than seven years. At the time, POWs were sometimes featured in **propaganda** films created by the Vietnamese government. The Vietnamese hoped that the prisoners would renounce US policy regarding Vietnam on camera and convince the world that they were being well treated.

But when Denton appeared in one such film, he instead turned the tables on his captors. During his interview, he reinforced his support for the US position in Vietnam. At the same time, he pretended to have a sensitivity to the floodlights shining on him—but in fact was blinking out the word *torture* in Morse Code. He provided US officials with the earliest confirmation that the Vietnamese were torturing him and the other American prisoners.

After his release, Denton was promoted to rear admiral. He later represented the state of Alabama in the US Senate.

In 1792, Charles Chappe devised a signaling system that was used extensively in France for both national and military communication before the invention of the telephone or electric telegraph.

Chappe's design involved towers topped with large crossbars with pivoting arms. Each crossbar had four arms, and each arm could be arranged in seven different positions to create different signals representing particular letters or words. To carry signals across greater distances than a single tower would allow, multiple towers were built from 5 to 20 miles apart. Tower operators watched the closest tower through spyglasses, and later telescopes, for a signal they then passed on to the next tower.

As Chappe's design was revised over the years, some operators replaced the crossbars with window shutters, which could be opened and closed to spell out the code. Eventually, flags replaced the earlier tower system, especially for naval activity. Signal flags have their disadvantages—messages were not secret unless operators used their own secret codes, and the flags could not be seen at night or in bad weather—but the US Navy still uses them today for certain communications.

The system Chappe originated uses the *position* of the flags to communicate—this is known as **semaphore**. But navies also communicate by using special flags to represent specific letters and words. They spell out messages by hoisting these flags on halyards, or ropes, specifically used for that purpose. One such system is the International Code of Signals, which is used by different naval forces, including the US Navy, to communicate with each other. Some navies also have additional flags and codes for their own needs.

As with other code and cipher systems, speed in communication is crucial. In the International Code of Signals, an individual flag or pennant can stand for a letter and be used to spell out words, but some flags also relay a specific message. For instance, the flag for *a*, which is called Alfa (or sometimes Alpha), also relays the message "I have a diver down; keep well clear at slow speed." And *o*, or Oscar, stands for "Man overboard." The full International Code of Signals alphabet is as follows:

a	Alfa/Alpha	m	Mike
b	Bravo	n	November
c	Charlie	o	Oscar
d	Delta	p	Papa
e	Echo	q	Quebec
f	Foxtrot	r	Romeo
g	Golf	s	Sierra
h	Hotel	t	Tango
i	India	u	Uniform
j	Juliet	v	Victor
k	Kilo	w	Whiskey
l	Lima	x	Xray
		y	Yankee
		z	Zulu

For more on this system, including the flag designs and the specific message associated with each one, see https://www.navy.mil/navydata /communications/flags/flags.html.

Quartermaster Seaman Robert Harry raises the *f*, or Foxtrot, flag on the forward mast, signaling the start of flight operations aboard the amphibious assault ship USS *Peleliu* (LHA 5). *Courtesy of the US Navy; the appearance of US Department of Defense (DoD) visual information does not imply or constitute DoD endorsement*

CREATE YOUR OWN FLAGS AND LEARN AND USE SEMAPHORE

In addition to the International Code of Signals, navies continue to use semaphore to communicate: flags are held by hand, and the position of the sender's arms spells out words. In this activity, you'll create your own flags to send a semaphore message.

YOU'LL NEED

- Pen or pencil
- 2 sheets of 8½-by-11-inch paper
- Ruler
- Crayons or markers
- Glue or glue stick
- 2 dowel rods, 24 inches long

1. Look at the semaphore chart on the next page. Notice the simple design of the flags, which helps them to be seen over long distances. Think about what colors would make them more visible. Today, nautical semaphore flags are yellow and red, while flags used on land are typically blue and white. Keep these things in mind when you're designing your own flag.

2. Draw a 1-inch margin on one side of each sheet of paper.

3. Create a design for your flag. Draw your design on one sheet of paper, with the margin on the left. Make your design to the right of the margin, using all the space outside of the margin.

4. Use crayons or markers to color your flag design.

5. Now create an identical flag on the second sheet of paper, but turn the paper so your design will be to the left of the margin.

6. For each flag, spread an even layer of glue in the entire margin.

7. Place a dowel rod on the glue, lining up the top edge of the rod with the top edge of the paper, and roll the rod and paper to the edge of your design. You might have to hold the paper in place for a while to allow the glue to set.

8. Set your flags aside until the glue is completely dry.

9. While you're waiting, think of a message you want to send. For instance, you could try to signal your name—a shorter message might be better for

your first try. Refer to the chart on the right to determine what positions to use to spell out your message. Positions are easy to visualize if you think of flags as pointing in the directions of the compass: north, northeast, east, southeast, south, southwest, west, and northwest.

10. When the glue on your flags is dry, hold them up so the designs face out.

11. Send your message to a friend, and have him or her use the chart to figure out what you're trying to communicate.

12. Store the flags in your Cryptologist's Kit, if they fit.

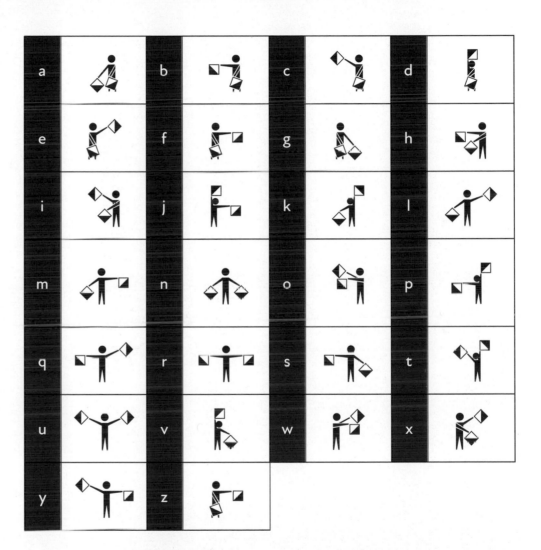

a commitment to clean air

7

HIDDEN...RIGHT BEFORE YOUR EYES...AND EARS

Have you ever noticed the zip code on a mailed envelope? Do you have any idea what those numbers mean? What about when you go shopping? Can you think of times when codes are used? Do you ever hear or see codes at school? If you pay attention, you might be surprised at how often you see or hear a code.

THE NEED FOR SPEED

Mail delivery in the United States has come a long way since its beginning on September 25, 1775. One of the biggest changes has been the zip code system, and now zip plus four. The *zip* in *zip code* stands for Zoning Improvement Plan. While zip codes helped speed up mail

Highway pictographs help travelers navigate more quickly. *Photo by author*

delivery, there is another reason zip codes became important. Although the use of zip codes was officially adopted in 1963, the idea was first discussed during World War II. With so many men and women involved in the war effort, the postal system faced a decrease in staff that negatively affected mail delivery.

Originally, a zip code consisted of two numbers. Today's zip code uses five numbers and, more often, nine. Zip code numbering begins in New England, with states such as Maine and Vermont having zip codes starting with zero. For states in the western part of the United States, such as California and Oregon, zip codes begin with nine. The states are grouped together into regions.

The next two digits of the code refer to smaller areas within the larger regions and, more specifically, to a central post office location for that area. Local post offices are represented by the last two numbers.

The plus-four numbers are used more and more and are specific to a delivery location. They were added to existing zip codes in 1983. Again, the reason was to increase efficiency. The sixth and seventh digits refer to a larger local area, such as a group of streets or post office box locations. The last two digits are specific to the actual delivery address.

Before the invention of computers, business owners usually kept track of sold or unsold items with paper and a pencil. Someone counted each item and recorded the information, sometimes monthly—a time-consuming process. This record of what a business has sold and what is still available to sell is known as an inventory. Not only does it help businesses determine when it's time to reorder products, but it also shows which items are not selling well and should be marked down in price or not reordered.

Today inventories are done at the cash register. This information—point of sale, or POS—does what business owners did for themselves, only more accurately and a lot faster. Inventories are updated immediately as items are sold. What makes this process work is a bar code or UPC (Universal Product Code). Bar codes might look like a row of random lines and numbers, but all that information has meaning, including the spacing between the lines and their thicknesses.

This zip code map shows zones in the United States. *Illustration by Denelson83, courtesy of the illustrator, via Wikimedia Commons, https://commons.wikimedia.org/wiki/File:ZIP_Code_zones.svg*

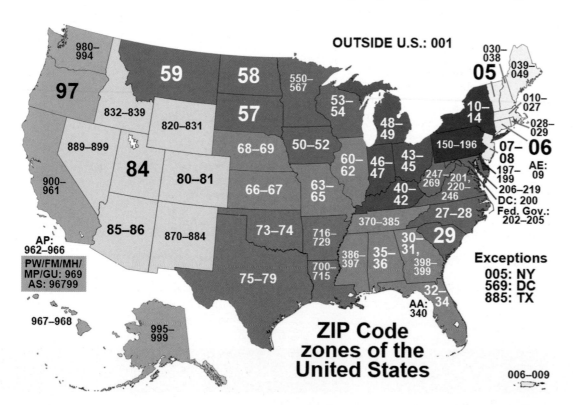

There are other bar code systems around the world to track purchases and inventory, but in the United States, Canada, and many other countries, the UPC system is used. Most people refer to UPCs as UPC codes, but when you think about it, that's like calling it a "Universal Product Code code"!

Besides tracking inventory, UPCs can be printed on sales receipts so customers and businesses know exactly what was purchased. This is especially important when you want to return an item. UPCs also are printed on coupons, which makes product discounts available at the time of purchase.

Some bar codes use a "compressed zero" format and have fewer than 12 digits, but usually bar codes include 12 digits. The first six identify the manufacturer, the next five identify the specific item, and the last one is called the check digit. The last number helps check that the other numbers have been scanned correctly. This is especially important if a scanner isn't working and numbers are entered manually. It would be easy to enter the wrong information.

The bars also play an important role, and while we usually see only the black ones, the white bars or lines are also important. There are four different bar widths in any UPC. Each bar's width represents a number value from one to four. What the UPC does not tell the cashier is price. This information is in the store's computer.

Whether you pay attention to bar codes or not, they're important for tracking which items are sold. When buying cheese, for instance, the UPC for a single package of cheese slices, a bag of cheese sticks, or a block of cheese—all sold by the same manufacturer—would each be different.

Where to Go and How to Arrive Safely

You can't walk down a street or drive in a car without seeing signs—traffic signs, storefront signs, signs about lost cats or upcoming yard sales. Traffic signs, like stop or yield signs, have words that tell you what to do. But why don't all signs use words? Why do some use a simple form of code called a **pictograph**?

Think about traveling in a car at 60 miles per hour. The driver needs to pay attention to traffic. But driving also means paying attention to what's around you—workers in the area, places to stop for gas, or cattle crossings. The sooner the driver gets the message, the better. And the quickest way to relay that information is through simple pictures.

Some state transportation departments use pictographs to convey information. One reason is that they help avoid issues with language barriers or reading ability. Another might be because studies have shown our brains register pictures 60,000 times faster than text. Pictographs can also be used internationally to share information.

Travel signs are posted well before highway exit ramps to alert travelers of what's ahead. Pictographs show where to find restaurants, gas stations, hotels, travel information, or other facilities ahead. Imagine if you needed a hospital. Seeing a universal sign for a hospital—a blue background with a large *H*—will make it much easier to get

Universal Product Codes keep track of products for manufacturers and retailers.

CHECK THE CHECK DIGIT

If for some reason a scanner isn't working properly and the cashier must enter the code by hand, it's easy for the cashier to make an error, especially if there are many items to check out. The check digit works exactly like its name says it does. It's a digit that works as a check on a product.

YOU'LL NEED

- Several items with 12-digit bar codes (food, clothing, games, toys)
- Calculator
- Paper
- Pen or pencil

1. Look at one 12-digit bar code.

2. Add up all the numbers that are in odd-numbered positions—the numbers in the first, third, fifth, seventh, ninth, and eleventh positions. Record that sum on your paper. Label it "Odd-numbered positions."

3. Multiply that sum by 3. Record that number on your paper as "Odd-numbered positions times 3."

4. Then add the numbers in the even-numbered positions, except for the check digit (the final digit). So, add up the numbers in the second, fourth, sixth, eighth, and tenth positions. Record that sum on your paper. Label it "Even-numbered positions."

5. Add together the number labeled "Odd-numbered positions times 3" and the number labeled "Even-numbered positions." Round this number up to the nearest 10s place (23 becomes 30, 49 becomes 50, 30 stays 30, etc.). Then subtract the original number from the rounded-up number. This number (7, 1, and 0 in the examples) should be the same as your check digit, the last number on the bar code.

6. You can also create your own bar code. Write down 11 numbers from 0 to 9. Leave off the check digit, since you don't know it yet.

7. Repeat steps 2 through 5, starting with finding the sum of the numbers in odd-numbered positions.

8. When you're done, figure out the number you need to add to your total to get a number divisible by 10. That's your check digit. You've created a bar code!

HIDDEN HELP FOR THOSE IN NEED

— — — — —

Hoboes, like these pictured, once traveled the country looking for work. *The George Grantham Collection of the Library of Congress, courtesy of Wikimedia Commons*

During difficult economic times, people used pictographs to communicate. During the Great Depression, which lasted from 1929 to 1939, many people were jobless and homeless. Survival often depended on the generosity of others.

Hoboes were homeless men and women, but they differed from tramps or bums because hoboes wanted to work. Many became hoboes because they lost their jobs. Often, they hopped trains to get from place to place, even though it was illegal and dangerous, to work on farms or in factories.

Hoboes sometimes established camps. It was common to see campfires burning, with makeshift tents to keep out rain and cold. Many camps were near railroads so hoboes had easy access to passing trains.

One way hoboes communicated was with symbols called hoboglyphs. Like other codes, these were meant to be secret. Since some hoboes couldn't read, pictures helped them find places to get a warm meal or sleep for the night, or served as a warning if the police were cracking down. Eventually, the hobo lifestyle became more of a choice than a necessity.

	Doctor here won't charge		Owners will give to get rid of you
	A kind lady lives here		Free telephone
	Barking dog here		Ill-tempered man lives here
	Bad water		Dangerous neighborhood
	Fresh water; safe campsite		A kind gentleman lives here

Hoboglyphs helped hoboes survive. They were like a universal language for hoboes that made their lives easier and helped them communicate. *Illustrations by Lindsey Cleworth Schauer, original images courtesy of the National Cryptologic Museum, National Security Agency*

there, especially in an emergency. Signs can show you where to find handicapped accessible restrooms, camping areas, safe drinking water, or trash barrels.

The colors and shapes of signs also communicate important information. Red is used for stop signs and sometimes yield signs. Orange indicates that there is work being done in an area so drivers know to be cautious. Yellow stands for a warning of some kind and is used for railroad crossings, changes in the direction of the road, or animals crossing ahead. Inverted triangular signs usually mean a driver must yield to other traffic. Green is used in the United States to indicate direction, such as route numbers, street names, and cardinal directions—north, south, east, and west. And when you're trying to find museums or historic places, watch for brown signs that are usually rectangular or square.

It's Smart to Be Prepared

Because of the need to be ready for any emergency, schools and communities have adopted codes used throughout the district or city. Police departments have their own codes as well. The codes help officers and trained personnel communicate quickly, which is crucial during an emergency. Police department code systems are often referred to as 10-codes.

The Association of Public Safety Communication Officials established the first 10-codes in 1940. These codes decreased the amount of verbal communication on radios and eliminated confusion. Another reason for 10-code systems is to keep radio transmissions more private and secure.

Some codes used by police are:

10-4	Message received
10-7	Out of service
10-10	Negative/no
10-14	Prowler report
10-18	Urgent
10-19	Return to the station
10-22	Disregard
10-26	Detaining suspect
10-51	Tow truck needed
10-52	Ambulance needed

Symbols like these communicate information to construction companies. Different colors indicate whether the underground lines are for telephones, alarm systems, gas, or oil. *Photo by author*

Some businesses use verbal codes to alert their employees to emergency situations. Say you're shopping at B&T's Clothing Store. If there's a problem with a shoplifter or an angry customer, the store doesn't necessarily want customers to know. You might hear announcements such as "Mrs. Brown, please move your car" or "Mr. Carson, your lights are on." These simple messages might be verbal codes that mean something else to the staff.

Some schools and communities prefer codes to relay important information in a short time. For instance, some schools use Code Red for an emergency that requires students to remain locked in their classrooms with their teachers. Code Yellow might indicate that students and teachers are to remain in their classrooms and assume normal activity, perhaps to reduce the amount of student traffic throughout the building. Most states now require regular lockdown drills.

Code Blue has become almost universally accepted for medical emergencies. It is used by police, first responders, and hospitals or medical facilities. Hospitals also use color codes. Again, sometimes they are used to alert personnel to emergency situations the hospital doesn't want the visiting public or patients to hear about.

Hospitals often refer to a Code Blue for an adult medical emergency and a Code White for a pediatric—or child's—medical emergency. Code Orange can alert staff to a hazardous waste spill, and Code Red is used extensively to indicate a fire.

HELP VISITORS NAVIGATE YOUR SCHOOL

Imagine that your school has invited students from another country to visit the school for a week of activities. Some of the students speak English, but others do not. The welcoming committee needs to make signs to help these visitors feel more comfortable and safer around your building. What kinds of signs will help these students navigate?

YOU'LL NEED

- Paper or poster board
- Pen or pencil
- Markers or crayons

1. Think of a list of places in your school where students go. Did you think of the lunchroom or school office?

2. On separate pieces of paper or poster board, draw a sign that might represent each of these places. What picture can you use to show the library or the nurse's room?

3. Show each sign to a classmate. Can he or she identify the locations? You don't want a visitor ending up in the library if he or she really needs to find a bathroom!

4. If visitors are coming to your school soon, such as for Grandparents' Day or another school event, ask your teacher about displaying your signs to help the visitors find their way around the school.

BE AWARE AND BE PREPARED: MAKE AN EMERGENCY PLAN FOR YOUR FAMILY

One idea behind using ciphers and codes is keeping people and information safe. When it comes to safety, family and friends top the list.

Do you know how to escape your home if there's a fire? Do you know where to go if your parents aren't home and there's a tornado? Do you know who to call if you become separated from your family? What would you do if a parent had a medical emergency? Every family should have an emergency plan in place. But what does that involve?

YOU'LL NEED

- Blank, unlined paper or graph paper
- Pen or pencil
- Roll of yarn or string
- Measuring tape or retractable tape measure
- Ruler (optional)

1. Think about situations that make up an emergency—a tornado or fire, for instance.

2. Make a drawing or map of all the rooms of your home. Try to make it as accurate as possible. Include the locations of doors and windows.

3. Visit every room. Can you see two ways out?

4. Tie a piece of string or yarn to a doorknob or a piece of furniture. Unroll the string until you reach a main door to get out of the house—usually the front, back, and/or side doors. Measure the unrolled length of string or yarn and record your measurement. Label it, such as "My bedroom to the front door" or "Upstairs bathroom to the back door."

5. Measure the distance from every room to every main door of your house.

6. Compare the measurements from each room to each door. Identify the shortest way out from each room. Record this information on the map.

7. Have a family emergency plan meeting. Share your escape map with your family.

8. Discuss where you would meet if there was a fire. Talk about where to go if there's a tornado or what to do if there's a flood. Be sure that everyone knows your street address and when to dial 9-1-1.

9. Discuss the names of two or three neighbors or relatives you can call if necessary. Agree on whom to call first so one person gets the information for all family members. Memorize those numbers and/or save them in your phone.

10. Agree on a code word that you can share with each other and the person you're calling so he or she knows it's really you and that you're safe.

11. In case of a *real* emergency, the most important thing is to get to safety and to call 9-1-1 if necessary. DO NOT hesitate to call 9-1-1, even if you forget your family's plan. SAFETY IS NUMBER 1!

12. If your phone call won't go through, try texting.

13. Run a drill and make changes to your map, escape plans, and/or people you'll call, if necessary. Practice your family emergency plan regularly.

QRs Deliver

Have you ever seen something that looks like this?

While bar codes are probably going to be around for a while, technology is constantly changing, and changing quickly. One of the newest ways to communicate involves QR (Quick Response) codes. In Japan, which is where QR codes were created, they're very common. First created in 1994 for the auto industry, they're actually a kind of two-dimensional bar code.

So, why go to the trouble of switching to QR codes? For one thing, a QR code can store more information than a bar code can. In addition to the information bar codes record, QR codes allow people to find information about a business or retrieve links to websites or geographic location information. But instead of needing a scanner, newer cell phones can scan and read QR codes with a simple point and click!

QR codes can also store bank or credit card information. They can be used to make payments or access coupons. QR codes can store 4,296 characters, whereas bar codes can only hold 12 characters. Plus, QRs are becoming more commonly used worldwide.

Whatever comes next, you can be sure new and different technology is already being created. Computers and electronic devices, and therefore codes and ciphers, continue to play a bigger role in our lives. They'll be part of *your* life even more.

8

NO ANSWERS IN SIGHT

There are still many ciphers and codes that remain unsolved. Some are related to military secrets, some hold clues to ancient civilizations, and some even hold information that might solve murders.

CLEVER CIPHERS IN ANCIENT TIMES

Buried in the peat bogs of Siberia, the Shigir Idol lay hidden for thousands of years. This 17-foot-tall wooden statue has since been confirmed to be about 11,000 years old. Because some pieces are missing, the idol may have actually been taller. As with ancient Roman tablets in England, the wood of the larch tree it was carved from, as well as its place in the bog, preserved the carving over the centuries. The larch tree that was used to carve the idol was 159 years old.

These 15 statues at Ahu Tongariki on Easter Island make up the largest group of moai anywhere.
Photo by Bjørn Christian Tørrissen, bjornfree.com, courtesy of the photographer

The straight lines on the idol may represent boundaries between earth and sky or might depict land or the horizon. Wavy lines are believed to be connected to travel, perhaps the direction to take to get to the end of a journey or even the number of days it might take to get there. Some may represent elements of nature, such as snakes or lizards. Geometric shapes likely stood for the sun or stars or other elements like fire.

Additional information about what the inscriptions mean continues to be discovered. For instance, researchers don't believe any part of the idol was buried in the ground. Then how did it stand up? One idea is that this two-story-tall carving was leaned vertically against a tree.

Researchers at the Yekaterinburg History Museum in Russia continue to study the idol for clues to its hidden meaning. Some believe it might be connected to totem poles originating with Native North Americans, who originally came from Siberia. Like many previous discoveries, deciphering the carving could reveal secrets about social classes, religions, and other aspects of the culture of people from long ago. Further research may uncover other secrets, but some experts caution that the lines might be more decorative in nature. But as researchers learn more about it, who knows what secrets the Shigir Idol might be hiding?

The photo at the beginning of this chapter shows the famous stone head statues of Easter

(left) The face of the Shigir Idol.
Siberian Times

(right) The body of the Shigir Idol shows definite signs of carvings.
Siberian Times

Island in the South Pacific. Surprisingly, it was recently discovered that some statues on the island have bodies that are hidden by soil and debris that built up over hundreds of years. This is not the only mysterious discovery related to the moai, as the statues were called by the Rapa Nui people who carved them.

Twenty-six wooden tablets covered with an unknown hieroglyphic alphabet were first discovered on Easter Island in 1868 by a Catholic missionary. The pattern on the tablets, or Rongorongo script, is considered by some to be based on an ancient language called the Old Rapa Nui language. Others believe it isn't a language at all but pictographic in nature. Images on the tablets show shapes and forms, including animals, humans, and unknown geometric shapes.

Some scholars believe decryption of the Rongorongo script might lead to clues about why this ancient civilization disappeared hundreds of years ago. Until then, the Rongorongo script remains a mystery. Maybe someday you'll be the one to solve it.

A similar mystery from southern Mexico is the Cascajal Stone, or Cascajal Block. This ancient slab of rock measures about 15 inches on its longest side and has six distinct surfaces or sides. Weighing just over 25 pounds, it is covered with 62 different images. Some scholars believe they're evidence of the earliest form of written language in the Western Hemisphere. The surface of the stone block might have been ground down so it could be reused. It will be interesting to see what discoveries await decryption.

Experts still do not agree on the meaning behind the unusual drawings, figures, and diagrams in the Voynich Manuscript. *Beinecke Rare Book & Manuscript Library, Yale University, courtesy of Wikimedia Commons*

Mysteries in History

One manuscript that remains a mystery today not only dates back over 600 years but also may hold the record for one of the longest at 232 pages. The Voynich Manuscript came to light in 1912 when Wilfrid Voynich, a book dealer, purchased it. Everything about this manuscript remains a mystery—the person who created it, the language it was written in, and the meaning of the text and illustrations throughout the book.

SAME TOOL, DIFFERENT RESULTS

Deciphering an ancient mystery can be challenging. But what one person can't figure out, another one might, and vice versa. In cryptology, different people can share the same tools or ideas and come up with entirely different ways to make or break a code or cipher. That's why people with different backgrounds have succeeded and continue to succeed as cryptanalysts.

YOU'LL NEED

- A friend
- Blank, unlined paper
- Pens or pencils

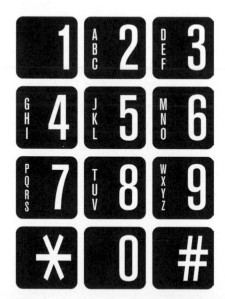

Illustration by Lindsey Cleworth Schauer

1. Look at the telephone keypad with a friend. Do you each see a connection between the numbers and letters? Keep what you notice to yourself and have your friend do the same.

2. Write individual messages you each want to encipher. Don't share them.

3. Study the keypad again. Can you think of a way to create a cipher using the keypad? It might have to do with the numbers and letters themselves. Or maybe you see something that has to do with the rows and columns on the keypad.

4. Once you have ciphers using the keypad, you should both encipher your messages.

5. Exchange your ciphered messages and try to solve each other's cipher. How did you do? Where you able to decipher your friend's message? Was he or she able to do the same?

6. If not, share your key with your friend or have him or her tell you his or her key. How different were your keys?

7. Can you come up with other ciphers using a telephone keypad?

There appears to be no logic to the placement of the text or the illustrations of unknown plants, diagrams, and small figures, which appear to be humans. Some people think the Voynich Manuscript is nothing more than a hoax. But that hasn't stopped some of the most expert cryptanalysts, including some from World Wars I and II, from trying to break the code. To date, all have failed.

Another story that captured the attention of the general public also remains a mystery. Like many unsolved codes and ciphers, some experts believe it's true, while others think it's a hoax. Either way, it's an interesting story.

The Beale ciphers have probably fueled more attention by amateur and professional cryptanalysts than any since Vigenère's cipher in 1586. According to one story, a stranger named Thomas J. Beale appeared in Lynchburg, Virginia, in the early 1820s. There he entrusted hotel owner Robert Morriss with a locked box. After the stranger left town, Morriss thought nothing more about the box until a letter arrived from Beale in May 1822. The letter claimed that in 1817, Beale and a group of about 20 men had discovered a gold mine while hunting buffalo, and that the box contained instructions on how to find it.

The twist was that the instructions were enciphered. The letter informed Morriss that if Beale or one of his men failed to retrieve the box within 10 years, Morriss himself should open it. In that case, a friend of Beale's would send Morriss a letter in June 1832, providing the key needed to decipher the instructions. Unfortunately, that letter never arrived.

Morriss waited until 1845. Then he broke the lock and opened the box, finding a plaintext note explaining why he was entrusted with it. Included were three enciphered sheets, covered with rows and rows of numbers. Here is a sample of the first two lines of the second Beale cipher:

115, 73, 24, 807, 37, 52, 49, 17, 31, 62, 647, 22, 7, 15, 140, 47, 29, 107, 79, 84, 56, 239, 26, 10, 811, 5, 196, 308, 85, 52, 160, 136, 59, 211, 36, 9, 46, 316, 554, 122

According to the plaintext note, the first enciphered sheet revealed the location of the treasure, the second gave details about it, and the third revealed the men's relatives who should be contacted to share the treasure.

Morriss decided it was time to find these relatives. After all, it had been 23 years since he had last seen Thomas Beale. But Morriss had no idea how to decipher the information. Try as he might, he never succeeded.

In 1862 Morriss trusted a friend, possibly named Ward, with the information. The friend attempted to decipher the texts. He assumed each number must stand for a letter. But since the ciphertext numbered into the thousands, he deduced it might possibly have been created using a book cipher.

In this type of cipher, each word in a text is numbered consecutively (1, 2, 3, etc.) and each number represents the first, or initial, letter of that word. After examining every book available to him, Ward finally stumbled on the Declaration of Independence as the key to the second ciphertext. Here is how a book cipher could be applied to the opening paragraphs of the Declaration of Independence. Each word is counted and numbered. Every fifth word is noted below, but from that it's easy to determine the number of every word by counting forward or backward:

When in the course ^{5}of human events, it becomes ^{10}necessary for one people to ^{15}dissolve the political bands which ^{20}have connected them with another, ^{25}and to assume among the ^{30}powers of the earth, the ^{35}separate and equal station to ^{40}which the Laws of Nature ^{45}and of Nature's God entitle ^{50}them, a decent respect to ^{55}the opinions of mankind requires ^{60}that they should declare the ^{65}causes which impel them to ^{70}the separation.

According to this cipher, the number 1 would stand for the letter *w* in an enciphered message (since that's the first letter of the first word, *When*), but so would the number 40 (since it's also the first letter of the 40th word, *which*). The numbers 3, 14, 16, 22, 26, 29, 32, 34, 39, 41, 50, 54, 55, 60, 61, 64, 68, 69, and 70 could all stand for the letter *t*.

In this way, Ward decrypted the second ciphertext, discovering valuable information about the supposed treasure. The text indicated that the treasure was buried in Bedford County, Virginia, about six feet below the ground, in iron pots with iron covers. It also claimed that the treasure included 2,921 pounds of gold and 5,100 pounds of silver, along with jewels. But Ward never found these riches, because he wasn't able to decrypt the first and third ciphers.

In 1885 Ward published a pamphlet about the mystery. He wrote that his involvement in trying to solve the cipher had brought him, and those under his safekeeping, nothing but heartache. Ward, too, gave up the search.

In the more than 100 years since the pamphlet was published, people have continued to try to crack the Beale cipher. Some people have worked equally hard to prove that Beale and Ward are the same person and it's all a giant hoax, while others believe it's possible the treasure was real but has already been found. However, many still believe that the Beale ciphers are real and that his treasure remains hidden. If you're one of them, maybe you could crack this mystery and find a treasure worth millions of dollars.

Not all unsolved codes and ciphers date back hundreds of years. More modern times have also yielded their share of mysteries. One of these dates back to 1935 and involves a four-time president of the United States, Franklin Delano Roosevelt.

At the time, William Friedman, later considered by many to be the Father of Cryptanalysis, gave lectures to cryptanalysts of the NSA. Part of his lectures, meant to inspire men and women about the importance of their work, included samples of different codes. One of the interesting things about the coded note that Friedman shared and President Roosevelt received was that one part was a transposition code and one part was a substitution code.

The transposition code was written as NDO-IMDEYLOAUEETVIEBR. To read the message, read every other letter from left to right beginning

CREATE A BEALE CIPHER

One of the strengths of the Beale cipher is that it uses a book or other text to determine the ciphertext. Think about it: frequency analysis wouldn't work, because you can use different numbers to represent the same letters. The more words in your writing sample, the more numbers you can use and the harder it will be to crack.

And while the cipher that was broken used a famous document, the Declaration of Independence, you can create a more challenging version by using something less common—for instance, an article in a local newspaper, or even something you yourself have written. That way, not everyone trying to decipher your message will have read that same text.

YOU'LL NEED

- A copy of a page from a favorite book or a newspaper article, at least 100 to 150 words long
- Pen or pencil
- Paper

1. Starting with the first word of the page or article, number each word consecutively. You can write every number before the first letter of every word, or every second or fifth or tenth word.

2. Write a message in plaintext on a separate sheet of paper.

3. Go through your numbered writing sample. Replace each letter of plaintext with a number corresponding to a word that begins with that same letter. You might have to change your message if it contains a letter not found in your writing sample.

4. Remember, for a friend to decipher your message, he or she needs to have the same key—the sample text—as you used to encipher it.

President Franklin D. Roosevelt receives a young visitor at his home in Hyde Park, New York. President Roosevelt was afflicted with polio in 1921 at the age of 39. *Photo by Margaret Suckley, courtesy of the FDR Presidential Library and Museum*

with the second letter and the remaining letters from right to left. (The answer can be found on page 117.)

After you decode it, here's a possible explanation about the meaning and why the code maker asked about a fruit. Roosevelt was confined to a wheelchair because of a disease called polio. At the time, people thought juice of the fruit mentioned in the message could help people with polio, so the belief is that part of the message referred to a treatment or cure for Roosevelt.

MURDER IN DISGUISE

Criminals and murderers also used codes. Gangs and other criminal groups still use them today. Gun smugglers, drug traffickers, and gangs—in prisons and on the streets—are interested in keeping their activities secret. In fact, today about 80 percent of the codebreaking efforts of the Cryptanalysis and **Racketeering** Records Unit (CRRU) of the Federal Bureau of Investigation (FBI) focuses on prison codes and ciphers.

In 1948 a dead body was found on Somerton beach in Australia. The Somerton Man, as he's been called, opened the door to a mystery still unsolved today.

Police immediately noticed several unusual things about the body found leaning against a seawall. For one thing, in spite of the hot weather, the man wore a knitted pullover sweater and a suit and tie. From his relaxed position, he could have been sleeping . . . except he was dead. And there was no indication of how he died and no recent reports of missing people.

In his pocket, police found a scrap of paper with the words *Tamám Shud* on it. *Tamám Shud* means "finished" in the Persian language. The torn scrap was actually the last page of a rare edition of *The Rubaiyat of Omar Khayyam*, a poetry

SHERLOCK HOLMES, FICTIONAL DETECTIVE

- - - - -

Police and other law enforcement officers work tirelessly to solve crimes. This is also the case for fictional detectives, such as Sherlock Holmes. Holmes was created by Sir Arthur Conan Doyle, whose first story involving the famous detective appeared in 1887. Like other successful cryptanalysts, Holmes possessed logical thinking skills and keen observation to solve crimes.

In Doyle's short story *The Adventure of the Dancing Men*, Holmes used frequency analysis to solve a substitution cipher of individual stick figures posed differently for each letter of the alphabet. Holmes also wrote an enciphered message using the Dancing Men cipher to lure and capture the villain in the story.

Illustrations by Lindsey Cleworth Schauer

Most of the stories take place between 1880 and 1914 and include Holmes's sidekick Dr. Watson. According to the *Guinness Book of World Records*, Holmes is the most frequently portrayed movie character in history. To many fans, Holmes is not a fictional character at all. Numerous fan clubs and literary societies exist worldwide, paying tribute to Britain's most famous detective.

book dating back to the 11th century. In place of the torn page was a list of random letters, which some people believe is a code of some kind. Along with the scrap of paper, chewing gum, a comb, and train and bus tickets were found in the man's pockets. His suitcase was found at a train station, but it yielded no helpful clues. Even a fingerprint search by the FBI gave no information.

After much research, detectives came up with the idea that the Somerton Man was actually a murdered Soviet or American spy. Will the mystery of the Somerton Man ever be solved? No one knows. But with advances in criminology and technology, this unknown person might someday have a name.

In 2011 codebreakers around the world were again called on to help solve a murder mystery, this one dating back to 1999. Prior to this, both the FBI's CRRU and members of the American Cryptogram Association had failed to solve the murder.

The victim found in St. Charles County, Missouri, was a 41-year-old man with intellectual disabilities and a past criminal history. Ricky McCormick lived with his mother, and at the time his body was found, no one suspected he had been murdered. It wasn't until almost 12 years later that investigators from the FBI decided to rethink their first conclusion.

Just like the Somerton Man, a search of McCormick's pockets turned up encrypted writing, only this time in the form of handwritten notes. Interestingly, while McCormick was involved in drug trafficking, he wasn't able to read or write. Some cryptanalysts believe he might have been dyslexic.

Were the notes found with McCormick written by someone else? Were they somehow linked to the drugs he had recently brought back from Florida? Or was there a connection with other criminals he was known to have associated with? At this point, no one knows. But the FBI has an address available for amateur and expert cryptanalysts who want to send in ideas on how to break the code. With luck, further investigation will reveal the clues to one of the CRRU's top unsolved crimes.

The enciphered note found on the body of Ricky McCormick. *US Federal Bureau of Investigation, courtesy of Wikimedia Commons*

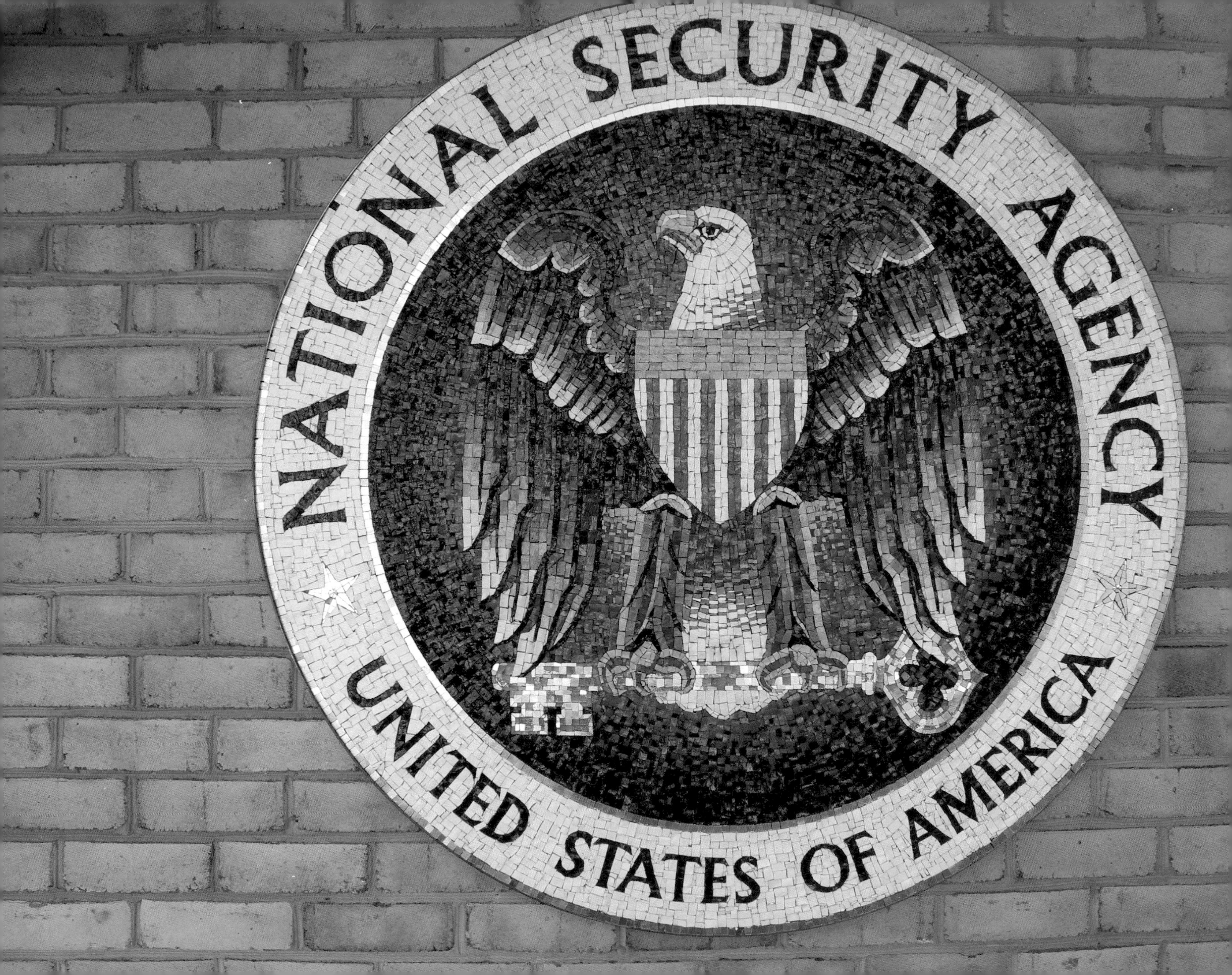
NATIONAL SECURITY AGENCY
UNITED STATES OF AMERICA

9

CODES AND CIPHERS IN A CHANGING WORLD

The mission of cryptology during wartime has changed little since people first used codes and ciphers thousands of years ago. Keeping sensitive information out of the enemy's hands was the goal of cryptologists then, and it's the goal of cryptologists now. But if you're not involved in a war, who is the enemy? In today's interconnected online world, that enemy could be anyone.

Cybersecurity refers to protecting electronic devices and programs, and the technology and information they contain, from someone else trying to gain unauthorized access to them. This includes both attempts to steal private information and attacks specifically designed to cause damage. Why is cybersecurity such a big deal? Because if you think about

The National Security Agency seal on display at the National Cryptologic Museum. *Photo by Buzz Daigneau, courtesy of the National Cryptologic Museum, National Security Agency*

it, millions of devices and programs we all use today are vulnerable to being accessed or attacked.

The Internet of Things

Today almost everything we use involves technology at some level. We all know that cell phones and other personal devices can connect us to banks, retailers, and social media pages with the tap of a few keys. But it goes beyond that: countless everyday objects, from refrigerators and other appliances to home security systems to automobiles, trucks, and motorcycles, have built-in computers or sensors that are accessible via the Internet. They make up what is known as the "Internet of things" (IOT).

Think about things you do almost every day. You eat, you sleep, you shower, you communicate with people. Many of these things involve using technology. And what's behind much of today's technology? Codes, mainly programming codes, created to help machines and sensors communicate with one another.

For example, cities need to prevent traffic accidents. What if cement was "smart," like smartphones and smart televisions? Actually, some cement is! Smart cement contains sensors that share data to report cracks, warps, or other defects. Smart cement signals to vehicles driving over it—smart cars—that ice has built up on a bridge. A smart car can read this technology and alert the driver to the upcoming hazard. And if the driver ignores the warning and doesn't slow down? Don't worry. The smart car will do that for him or her.

It's encryption of information or data that allows that to happen.

Technology helps the world grow crops more efficiently, stay on top of weather emergencies, and keep us safe inside our homes and out. Smart refrigerators now scan bar codes to keep track of the food stored inside and when it's going bad. Smart toilets clean themselves. And future wearable devices will automatically adjust room lighting and temperature to the wearer's needs.

But with all these devices constantly exchanging data, private citizens and organizations worldwide need to work hard to keep them secure.

Who's Doing Something About Cybersecurity?

In the United States, the CIA, FBI, and NSA are just some of the government agencies dealing with cybersecurity problems. The NSA is housed in a two-million-square-foot facility, one of the most secret and secure places in the country, where it monitors millions of e-mails, cell phone conversations, and other means of communication, watching for anything that might pose a threat to the United States. Its goal is to gather information, defeat threats, and protect American interests.

After the terrorist attacks of September 11, 2001, the focus of the NSA changed forever. While many of its more than 40,000 civilian employees worldwide are responsible for monitoring threats within the United States, that single event changed the agency's focus to events outside the United

EVERYDAY ITEMS IN DISGUISE

— — — — —

Even before the development of the Internet of things, espionage experts could tinker with everyday objects to help them gather or protect secret information. These objects, called concealment devices (CDs), look like everyday items but have another purpose. During World War II, one unusual concealment device was the board game Monopoly.

The idea came from a British intelligence officer named Christopher Clayton Hutton, who created CDs to smuggle into German POW camps to help the prisoners escape. Hutton was familiar with a company called John Waddington Limited, which produced silk maps that were sewn into soldiers' uniforms. The risk of them being discovered was lower because silk doesn't crinkle like paper. The same company had also been printing Monopoly in England since around 1935.

Hutton contacted the company chairman with his idea: hide POW escape kits inside copies of Monopoly. The game board's ⅛-inch thickness made it perfect for hiding a silk map, a file, a small compass, and a small wire saw. Real money could be hidden among the game's fake money.

The games were manufactured and sent to German POW camps. The Germans let prisoners receive care packages from family members and support organizations, believing games and other personal items kept the prisoners too busy to plan escapes. But almost 750 pilots and airmen escaped using devices created by Hutton and his US partner, Captain Robley Winfrey. They created other games, baseballs, and chess sets. While most items were discovered, the Monopoly games never were.

Another clever CD spied on the US government: a carved wooden replica of the Great Seal of the United States. It was gifted to the US ambassador to the Soviet Union, Averill Harriman, in 1946 by a group of Russian schoolchildren, as an expression of friendship to one of Russia's allies during World War II. Or at least that's what people, including Harriman, thought for years. Although the carving was checked for spy gadgets, it contained a hidden listening device that wasn't discovered until US and British military radio operators overhead the voice of the ambassador to Russia while listening to Russian radio communications.

By that point, the seal had hung in Ambassador Harriman's Moscow office for seven years. Without batteries or a power pack, a small wire membrane inside vibrated and sent signals to listening Russian agents across the street. It was virtually impossible to detect.

A replica of the Great Seal of the United States presented to Ambassador Averill Harriman.
Photo by Buzz Daigneau, courtesy of the National Cryptologic Museum, National Security Agency

MAKE A SECRET BOOK COMPARTMENT

Cryptology is all about keeping information hidden, and spies have been using steganography as one way to do this. Buttons and hollow heels in shoes were used to hide coded messages, as were common items like cigarette lighters, table lamps, ballpoint pens, and makeup cases. The need to hide messages became so important that after World War II, the US Central Intelligence Agency (CIA) established the Office of Technical Services (OTS) to develop disguises, adapt everyday items, and create new technologies to keep communications secret.

ADULT SUPERVISION REQUIRED

YOU'LL NEED

- Old book that is no longer needed
- Ruler
- Pen or pencil
- Craft knife

1. Open the book to somewhere near the middle.

2. With the ruler and pen or pencil, draw a rectangle in the middle of the right-hand page, leaving a margin between the sides of your rectangle and the edges and middle of the book.

3. *Carefully* use the craft knife to cut through several pages, following the drawn lines of the rectangle. Do not try to cut through all the pages at once, just a few.

4. To make the hidden compartment deeper, flip through several cut pages, leaving one as a guide. Cut through additional pages.

5. Leave a number of uncut pages at the front and back of the book.

6. Hide a secret message or item inside the compartment you just made and then close the book.

7. If it fits, add your book to your Cryptologist's Kit.

These buttons, from pants worn by members of the Royal Australian Air Force, could be put together to make a compass. *Courtesy of the Auckland Museum, via Wikimedia Commons, https://commons.wikimedia.org/wiki /File:Compass,_button_(AM_2004.41.4-1) .jpg*

States—namely, terrorism. But, don't forget that while the NSA is trying to gather information, those working against it are working equally hard to keep that information secret.

Linguists working at the NSA are trained in several languages, and up to 130 languages are monitored. These language specialists are also trained to recognize voices. That might involve listening for words out of character for a particular person. But it doesn't always mean listening to *what* someone says; it might be as simple as *how* someone says it.

Whether it's a government agency or someone in the **private sector**, security experts work hard to keep us safe. Information Security Officer John Brozycki's work in the financial industry involves using and monitoring encrypted passwords, secure e-mails and web browsing, and private and business networks.

He notes how the increased use of computers and mobile devices today makes everyone open to trouble. With so many IOT devices available—cameras, appliances, thermostats—we're all at risk. "All of these rely on encryption and the underlying ciphers to protect those communications and data sets," Brozycki notes. He goes on to explain, "We all use them whether we realize it or not, as ciphers are key for secure electronic communications."

THE CIA'S PUBLIC SECRET

- - - - -

One secret that the CIA encourages the public to discover is the message that remains hidden on a sculpture titled *Kryptos* by artist James Sanborn. It stands outside the agency's headquarters in Langley, Virginia. Dedicated in November 1990, the sculpture includes petrified wood to represent trees that once grew on the spot, a small bubbling pool to symbolize information released in the world, and a copper screen with exactly 1,735 letters covering its surface. Among the characters on the sculpture are a copy of Vigenère's tableau and some Morse code.

Four coded messages are contained in the sculpture, and to date only three have been solved. The first message is a phrase that Sanborn created, but it contains a misspelling. The second message hints at something buried, perhaps on CIA grounds but possibly elsewhere. The last message includes a quote about the opening of King Tut's tomb in 1922 from archaeologist Howard Carter's diary.

But it's the fourth riddle—referred to as K4—that still stumps the world's greatest cryptanalysts today.

Of the 97 letters in K4, 86 remain unsolved. In 2010 Sanborn gave a clue to six of the letters, which spell the word *Berlin*. More recently, he revealed the next word, which is *clock*. Besides deciphering the text, the last piece to the puzzle is finding the answer to the riddle. Only Sanborn, with help from a retired CIA cryptographer, knows the solution.

The *Kryptos* sculpture at the US Central Intelligence Agency's headquarters. *Kryptos* means "hidden." *Sculpture by James Sanborn, courtesy of the artist*

A New Approach to an Old Problem

As computers continued to evolve in the 1970s, the need to deal with changes in how they communicated with each other became more obvious. Fortunately, cryptologists set their sights on where the technology was headed.

One of the issues that needed to be addressed was called the **key exchange**. At the time, security depended on keys that were **symmetric**, which means enciphering and deciphering used the same key or closely related keys. Every customer who wanted to use a credit card to purchase an item from a business, let's say a book, would need a unique key provided by that business for the transaction to be secure. This becomes difficult when there are thousands or even millions of customers. Getting the keys into all those people's hands would be a big obstacle.

Finally, in 1976, the idea of **public key cryptography** was put forth. In such systems, everyone wanting to send a credit card number to a business to make a purchase could use that company's key. That is, there's a single key that the company makes available to everyone. This is called the **public key**. It's used for enciphering all the messages that the thousands or millions of people need to send. The company also has a single private key, which is completely different from the enciphering key. This private key is kept secret by the company and used for deciphering every message it receives. With this kind of system, the company only needs one set of keys for all of its customers.

It took three computer science researchers at the Massachusetts Institute of Technology to come up with a public key cipher called RSA. The name came from the initials of their last names—(Ronald) Rivest, (Adi) Shamir, and (Leonard) Adleman. The researchers' efforts brought about the creation of public key cryptography. The difference with RSA was that both the public and the private keys could be used to encrypt and decrypt information.

Today there are greater demands on encryption. Encrypting information has three main purposes: to keep information safe from others, to prevent anyone from changing that information, and to be able to confirm without a doubt that you are communicating with the person or entity with whom you want to communicate and for that person or entity to confirm the same thing.

Modern encryption methods are usually described as having a certain number of keys, consisting of a certain number of **bits**. But instead of using numbers from zero to nine, bits are written as zeros and ones. In the case of a 128-bit cipher, the size that is most commonly used and is fairly secure, 128 zeros and ones are used, which translates to a 39-digit number. If you were going to try each combination in that key to unscramble the information, it would take 340,000,000,000,000,000,000,000,000,000,000,000,000 tries to do that. Compare that to a four- or five-bit cipher like Caesar's cipher, which has 26 possible key combinations. You can understand why information that needs heavy-duty protection uses even larger bit keys.

But how does this all work in the world? Fortunately, a cipher called AES (Advanced Encryption

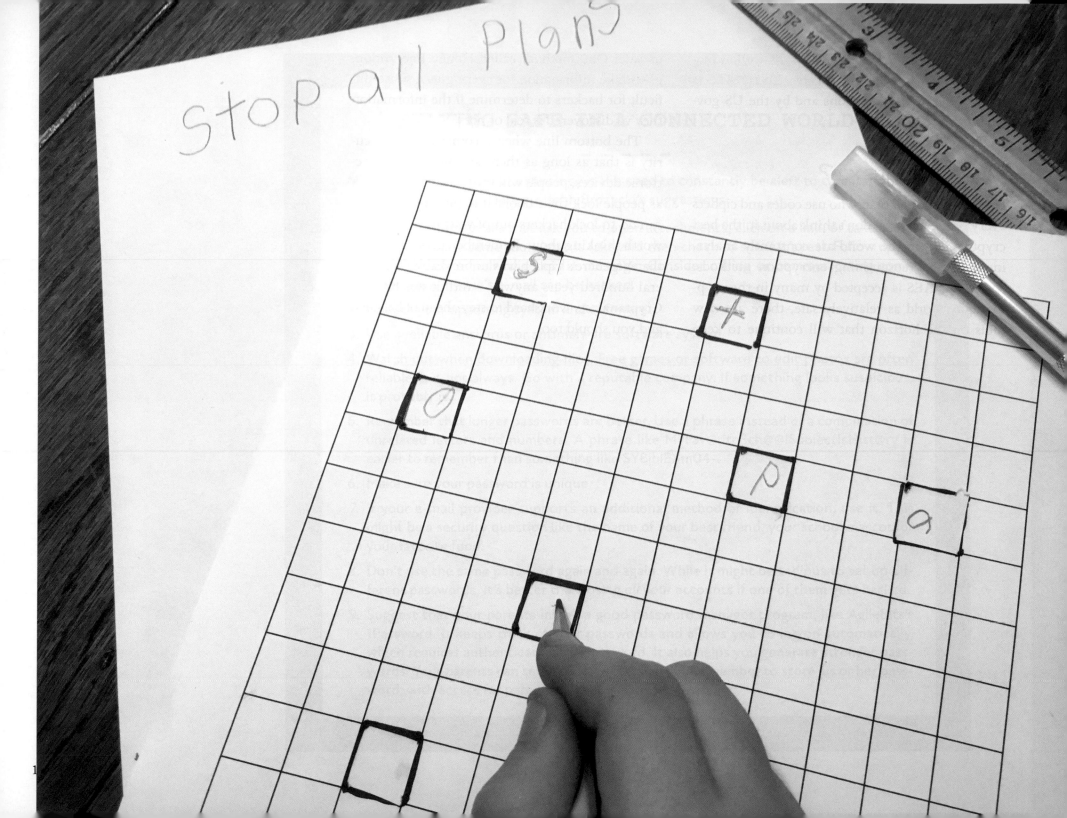

BE A CODE AND CIPHER CHAMP

By now you've learned a lot about the history of codes and ciphers and how they fit into the world years ago and today. You probably also know enough to be a code and cipher champ. This chapter will show you other ways to boost those skills. You will need paper and a pen or pencil for these codes and ciphers.

TIPS FOR SOLVING CODES AND CIPHERS

Solving codes and ciphers before computers were invented meant looking at words, recognizing patterns in them, and thinking about letter relationships. Sometimes it was just about making guesses. Here are few tips:

1. Use a pencil; it's a lot easier to erase!
2. Study the enciphered text before jumping in. What kind of code or cipher is it? Look for word patterns. Do you see words that stand out by reading, say, every second letter? Or do you recognize words that might be written backward or in some reversed or scrambled order?
3. Look for one-letter words that stand alone. Unless the ciphertext is followed by a period, such as for an initial, the letter must be *a* or *i*.
4. If you find one-letter words, look for other places those letters might appear. For instance, the letter *i* spells a common one-letter word but rarely appears at the end of longer words (with exceptions such as *ski*, *lei*, and *obi*), especially not two-letter words.
5. Look for two-letter words. Most include a vowel and a consonant.
6. Look for the same two letters in combination. The most commonly used same two-letter combinations are *ll*, *ss*, *ee*, and *tt*.
7. Look for three-letter words. The most common in the English language are *the* and *and*.
8. Look for apostrophes. Common single letters following apostrophes are *s*, *t*, *d*, and *m*. The most common two-letter word combinations following an apostrophe are *ll* and *re*.
9. Use the charts on page 8 to recognize two- or three-letter combinations.
10. The most common four-letter word that begins and ends with the same letter is *that*.
11. What other word rules do you know?
12. Take a guess. You might be wrong, but you might also be right!

PIGPEN CIPHER

Some people believe the pigpen cipher was used about 800 hundred years ago, during the Crusades, which were religious wars involving the Catholic Church. The pigpen cipher lost its popularity until early in the 18th century when members of fraternal societies—clubs whose members shared common interests and beliefs—started using it again. One of these organizations was the Freemasons, so this cipher is also called the Freemason cipher.

As you look at each letter, study the lines and dots around it. Each cipher letter takes on these individual features. The word *cipher* is shown as an example.

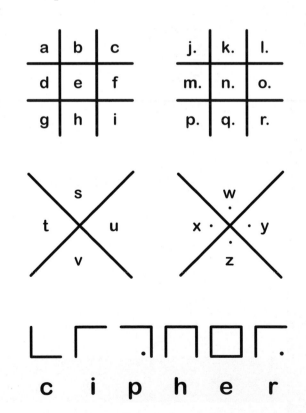

Tic-Tac-Toe Cipher

This cipher is like the pigpen cipher, but instead of using an X-shaped grid for some letters, it only uses a tic-tac-toe grid. As you'll see, the number of dots is important. A different version of this cipher was used by another fraternal organization called the Rosicrucians.

The word *cipher* is shown as an example.

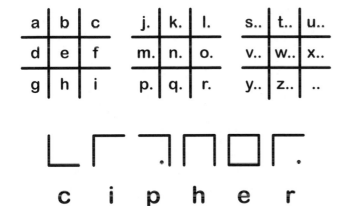

Date Shift Cipher

The trick to this cipher is that the key can be something easy to remember. After all, it's not very likely you'll forget your birthday, right? This key uses a simple month-day-year format.

First, write a message in plaintext. Then decide what key you're going to use. This example uses July 4, 1776. Write the key in numbers and eliminate the hyphens, putting a zero at the beginning of the first nine days of the month and the first nine months of the year. You always want to write the dates and months as two digits. So, the sample key would be 07041776. Write the alphabet separately in correct order with the key beneath it. This will get you started:

a	b	c	d	e	f	g	h	i	j	k	l	m	n	o	p	q	r	...
0	7	0	4	1	7	7	6	0	7	0	4	1	7	7	6	0	7	...

Let's use the word *cipher* again. To encipher this word, shift each letter by the number of places designated by the date number under that letter. For *cipher*, the *c* would not be shifted because of the zero, and the *i* would also not be shifted. The *p* would be shifted six places, and so on. If you get to the *z* at the end of the alphabet, wrap around to the *a* to shift. Here's what *cipher* would look like in ciphertext: CIVNFY.

Split-Rail Fence Cipher

This simple cipher uses the framework of a split-rail fence to encipher a message. It's an easy transposition cipher that dates back to the Civil War.

First write a message that you want to encipher. Then draw a split-rail framework as shown to the right. Write each letter of your message on the points of the "fence," starting at the upper left point, then moving to the bottom left point, then the next upper point, and back and forth. Each point should have one letter. Draw another split-rail fence if your message is long.

To convert your message into ciphertext, write out all the letters on the top points of the rail in

Split rail framework.

MAKE A CARDANO GRILLE

A grille, or mask, is a paper with holes or squares cut into it. Girolamo Cardano, an Italian mathematician and doctor, is credited with inventing this way of sending a secret message. Instead of using a code or cipher to disguise a message, the message itself is hidden in a longer message that could be as simple as a note to a friend!

ADULT SUPERVISION REQUIRED

YOU'LL NEED

- ◉ Pen or pencil
- ◉ Sheet of graph paper with a 1-inch grid
- ◉ Craft knife
- ◉ 1 or 2 sheets of blank, unlined paper

1. Draw 10 to 12 squares anywhere on the graph paper. Don't make any squares on the edges of your paper, and allow at least one square between the squares you draw.

2. With a craft knife, *carefully* cut out each square or window.

3. Optional: Number under each square in any order. This will make your message a little harder to decipher.

4. Write a message you want to send.

5. Place your grille on top of a separate sheet of unlined paper. Write your message, one letter in each square, following the order of the numbering you used above, or simply write one letter in each square from left to right. For a long message, you can use a separate sheet of paper and even turn the grille first.

6. Remove the grille and fill the spaces in between the letters, writing any message you like.

7. When you send your message, your friend will need the same Cardano grille to read it as you used to create it.

8. If you plan to reuse it, store your grille in your Cryptologist's Kit.

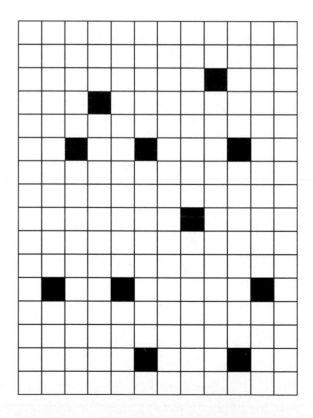

order, and then all the letters on the bottom points in order. The words *cipher champ* would be enciphered as CPECAP IHRHM.

By plugging the letters into the same zigzag framework in reverse—the first half of the cipher on the top points and the second half of the cipher on the bottom—your message can be deciphered.

CLOCK CIPHER

This is a simple cipher that's based on the face of an analog clock—a clock with moving hands. Each letter corresponds to a different time on the clock, except for letters *y* and *z*.

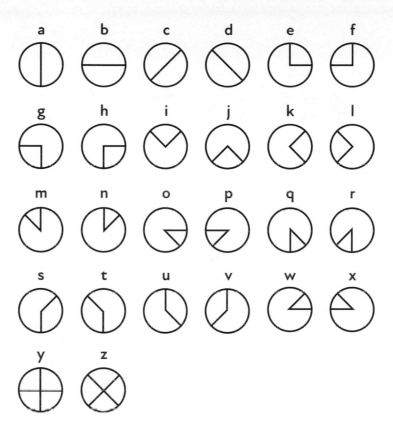

PUT YOUR SKILLS TO THE TEST

By now you should be fairly good at solving codes and ciphers. Here's a final message for you. This kind of cipher is called a cryptogram when it appears in puzzle magazines. Using the different codes and ciphers you've learned in Code Cracking for Kids, *can you decipher it?*

The best way to get started is to rewrite the cipher on blank paper. Just as you've done before, write the plaintext letters above the enciphered letters as you figure them out. Since some codes and ciphers use the same symbol for different letters, how should you start? Try looking at letters that you know belong to a specific code or cipher system. The more letters you decipher, the easier it will be to figure out the others. The answer key and the deciphered message are on page 117.

⅄ ··−·   ⟨ 34 54

31 ◐ 10   ╪ U Dzeh ◐ Kilo

⌐ ∞ ⅄ ⌠   31 ⅄ ◪ ∞ Dzeh U ,

⟨ 34 54   ⌐ U 54 Lima ⟨

◐ U Dzeh   ◐   31 34 ♯ Dzeh

◐ 10 ♯   31 ⅄ ◪ ∞ Dzeh U

31 ∞ ◐ ◪ ◪ !

GLOSSARY

— — · / · — · · / — — — / · · · / · · · / · — / · — / — · — —

Antimalware A software tool used to detect and protect from malware, software that targets computers and information technology systems with the purpose of causing damage or gaining unauthorized access.

Antivirus A tool used to detect and protect against computer viruses.

Bit A shortened term for "binary digit," which is the smallest measure of computer data and is assigned a value of 0 or 1.

Black chamber A government group that mostly operates in secret, usually to decipher or decode messages.

Cartouche A loop that surrounds other symbols—usually foreign words—in hieroglyphics.

Cipher A system of secret writing in which letters, numbers, or symbols replace individual letters, combinations of letters, or numbers.

Cipher disk A device consisting of two different-sized disks used for encoding and decoding.

Ciphertext A message as it appears once it's been rewritten or reproduced in code or cipher form.

Code A system of secret writing in which letters, numbers, symbols, or words replace whole words or phrases.

Conspirators People working together in secret, usually against a government or legal entity, for a specific shared purpose.

Cryptanalysis The process of decoding or deciphering a message without a key.

Cryptologist A person who makes and breaks codes and ciphers.

Cryptology The study of codes and ciphers.

Cybersecurity Steps or processes taken to protect electronic data.

Dead drops Specific locations, such as a bus station or farm field, where secret information is left to be picked up by someone else.

Declassified Indicates previously secret documents that have been released by a government after being deemed safe for public knowledge; in the United States classified documents are usually declassified after 25 years.

Decode To determine what a message written in code means.

Decipher To determine what a message written in cipher means; also referred to as *decrypt*.

Decrypt To determine what a message written in cipher means; also referred to as *decipher*.

Demotic A simple cursive form of writing used by the Egyptians.

Dichotomic Something divided into two separate parts, such as a dichotomic chart used to teach Morse code, with separate sides for dots and dashes.

Digraph Two letters that combine to make one sound.

Diplomatic Indicates something (a document, a person, etc.) that pertains to a country's relationship with other nations (for instance, a note exchanged between a government and its representatives in another country is referred to as a *diplomatic message*).

Double agent A person who pretends to be working for one group of people or one entity, often a government, but who reports confidential information to that group's enemies.

Encode To take a plain message and rewrite or reproduce it in code.

Encipher To take a plain message and rewrite or reproduce it in a cipher; also referred to as *encrypt*.

Encrypt To take a plain message and rewrite or reproduce it in a cipher; also referred to as *encipher*.

Espionage Secret activity, usually carried out on behalf of a government and often behind enemy lines.

Frequency analysis A decoding or decrypting technique that compares the most commonly used letters in a language to the mostly commonly used letters in a coded or ciphered message in order to solve the code or cipher.

Hieroglyph An individual picture or symbol used in an Egyptian form of writing to replace a word, letter, or syllable.

Hieroglyphic An Egyptian form of writing that uses pictures or symbols for words, letters, or syllables.

Key The secret guidelines that indicate how a particular code or cipher can be decoded or decrypted.

Key exchange A process of sharing a key between both a sender and a receiver, while protecting it from others not authorized to use it.

Keyword A word that serves as the key for making and breaking a code or cipher.

Linguists People who study languages.

Monoalphabetic cipher A cipher that is written using only one alphabet.

Nomenclator A system that uses both code words and a cipher alphabet for enciphering a message.

Nulls Symbols, words, or letters that have no meaning to a specific message but are included to fill in spaces or to make decoding and deciphering more difficult.

Pictograph A picture used for communication.

Plaintext A message as it appears before it's been rewritten or reproduced in code or cipher form.

Polyalphabetic cipher A cipher that uses more than one alphabet.

Private sector The part of a country's economy that is not owned or controlled by the government.

Propaganda Information, usually false, distributed by a government or entity to publicize or promote a particular belief, event, or point of view.

Public key A key that is used to encrypt information and that is available to the public.

Public key cryptography A system of cryptography that incorporates a public key for encryption and a private key for decryption.

Racketeering Engaging in illegal business, often organized by a particular group and related to gambling or drugs.

Reagent A substance applied to invisible ink to cause the letters and words to appear.

Rebus A puzzle in which pictures or symbols replace words.

Scripts Systems of writing.

Scytale A rod or cylinder wrapped in leather or parchment and written on with the purpose of sending a secret message.

Semaphore A system that uses the position of a flag or similar object to communicate messages over long distances.

SIGABA A machine used by the United States from World War II until the 1950s to encrypt messages.

Steganography A method for preventing something, especially a secret message, from being discovered simply by hiding it—for instance, inside a button or in the hollow heel of a soldier's shoe.

Substitution code/cipher A code or cipher that replaces the symbols, letters, numbers, or words in a plaintext message with other symbols, letters, numbers, or words to create the coded or ciphered message.

Symmetric In cryptography, describes a system that uses the same key for encrypting and decrypting.

Transposition code/cipher A code or cipher that rearranges the symbols, letters, numbers, or words in plaintext message to create the coded or ciphered message.

ANSWERS REVEALED

-- --/.../--- /./.-./.../.-/./.--/./.-/.--./.-/.--...

Frequency Analysis riddle (Chapter 1): **What secret message did the snowman write? It's code out here!**

Franklin Delano Roosevelt letter (Chapter 8): **Did you ever bite a lemon**

Put Your Skills to the Test (Chapter 10): **If you can break this cipher, you truly are a code and cipher champ!**

Symbol		Symbol		Symbol		Symbol		Symbol	
⊘ Clock cipher	a	Dzeh — Navajo alphabet	e	Kilo — International Code of Signals alphabet	k	34 — Polybius square	o	⊔ Tic-tac-toe cipher	t
‡ Mary, Queen of Scots	b	..-. Morse code	f	Lima — International Code of Signals alphabet	l	Semaphore	p	54 — Tap code	u
31 — Tap code	c	∞ Mary, Queen of Scots	h	Semaphore	m	U — Caesar cipher	r	< Pigpen cipher	y
♯ Washington's code	d	Dancing Men cipher	i	10 — Beale cipher	n	Hieroglyphics	s		

WEBSITES AND PLACES TO VISIT

--—/·/-···/···/·/-/·/···/·-/-·/-·/·--—/·--/·-/--·-/·/···/-/---/···-/·/···/··/-

The Black Chamber by Simon Singh
http://www.simonsingh.net/The_Black_Chamber/

Central Intelligence Agency, Langley, VA
https://www.cia.gov/about-cia/headquarters-tour/

Central Intelligence Agency Kids' Zone
https://www.cia.gov/kids-page

Crypto Corner
https://crypto.interactive-maths.com/

Cryptogram Corner
http://cryptogramcorner.org/

Enigma Simulation
http://enigmaco.de/enigma/enigma.html

George Washington's Mount Vernon: The Culper Code Book
https://www.mountvernon.org/george-washington/the
-revolutionary-war/spying-and-espionage/the-culper-code-book/

International Spy Museum, Washington, DC
https://www.spymuseum.org/

Morse Code Translator
https://morsecode.scphillips.com/translator.html

National Cryptologic Museum, National Security Agency, Fort Meade, MD
https://www.nsa.gov/about/cryptologic-heritage/museum/

NOTES

−·/−−−/−/·/···

Introduction
"The necessity of": Wall text, "George Washington," National Cryptologic Museum, National Security Agency, Fort Meade, MD.

1. What Is Cryptology?
"I only regret": George Washington's Mount Vernon, "American Spies of the Revolution," accessed February 3, 2018, http://www.mountvernon.org/george-washington/the-revolutionary-war/spying-and-espionage/american-spies-of-the-revolution/.

"varying the angles": Dr. Roger Tomlin, e-mail interview by Jean Daigneau, January 23, 2018.

3. Colonies United
"sympathetic stain": George Washington's Mount Vernon, "Spy Techniques of the Revolutionary War," accessed May 24, 2019, https://www.mountvernon.org/george-washington/the-revolutionary-war/spying-and-espionage/spy-techniques-of-the-revolutionary-war/.

"Write no more": Singh, *The Code Book*, 80.

4. States Divided
"You have sent": Lineberry, "Elizabeth Van Lew," https://www.smithsonianmag.com/history/elizabeth-van-lew-an-unlikely-union-spy-158755584/.

5. The World Goes to War
"For God's sake": Robertson, "Revealed," https://www.dailymail.co.uk/news/article 3456252/How-messenger-dog-called-Satan-dodged-German-fire-gas-mask-help-Allied-forces-turn-tide-one-Great-War-s-bloodiest-battles.html.

6. Breaking the Unbreakable
"Maybe I was": Gentzke, "An American Hero," http://www.buffalo.edu/atbuffalo/article-page-spring-2018.host.html/content/shared/www/atbuffalo/articles/Spring-2018/features/an-american-hero.detail.html.

"Many seeds are": CBS This Morning, "Secret Code," https://www.cbsnews.com/news/secret-code-within-wwii-pows-letters-cracked-70-years-later/.

"every single night": Sisk, "Vietnam Era POW," https://www.military.com/daily-news/2016/09/16/vietnam-era-pow-demonstrates-tap-code-at-pow-mia-ceremony.html.

9. Codes and Ciphers in a Changing World
"All of these": John Brozycki, CISSP, e-mail interview by Jean Daigneau, May 30, 2018.

SELECTED BIBLIOGRAPHY

∙∙∙/∙/−∙∙/∙/−−∙/−/∙/−∙∙/−∙∙∙/∙∙/−∙∙∙/∙−∙∙/∙∙/−−−/−−/∙−/∙−/−−∙/∙∙∙∙/−∙−−

Aaseng, Nathan. *Navajo Code Talkers*. New York: Walker and Company, 1992.

Blackwood, Gary. *Mysterious Messages*. New York: Dutton Children's Books, 2009.

Blake, Spencer. *Spyology: The Complete Book of Spycraft*. Somerville, MA: Candlewick Press, 2008.

Brook, Henry. *Spying*. London: Usborne Publishing Limited, 2013.

CBS This Morning. "Secret Code Within WWII POW Letters Cracked 70 Years Later." July 25, 2013. https://www.cbsnews.com/news/secret-code-within-wwii-pows-letters-cracked-70-years-later/.

Doyle, Arthur Conan. "The Adventure of the Dancing Men." Orig. publ. 1859. Via the Arthur Conan Doyle Encyclopedia, last updated October 30, 2018. https://www.arthur-conan-doyle.com/index.php?title=The_Adventure_of_the_Dancing_Men.

Gentzke, Anne Whitcher. "An American Hero: Genevieve Grotjan Applied Her Dazzling Mathematical Skills to Unraveling Enemy Codes During World War II." *At Buffalo*, Spring 2018. http://www.buffalo.edu/atbuffalo/article-page-spring-2018.host.html/content/shared/www/atbuffalo/articles/Spring-2018/features/an-american-hero.detail.html.

Goldstone, Lawrence, and Nancy Goldstone. *The Friar and the Cipher*. New York: Doubleday, 2005.

Guinness World Records News. "Sherlock Holmes Awarded Title for Most Portrayed Literary Human Character in Film & TV." May 14, 2012. http://www.guinnessworldrecords.com/news/2012/5/sherlock-holmes-awarded-title-for-most-portrayed-literary-human-character-in-film-tv-41743/.

Hossell, Karen Price. *Ciphers and Codes*. Chicago: Heinemann Library, 2003.

Janeckzo, Paul. *Top Secret: A Handbook of Codes, Ciphers, and Secret Writing*. Somerville, MA: Candlewick Press, 2004.

Kahn, David. *The Code Breakers. The Story of Secret Writing*. New York: Scribner, 1967.

Kilmead, Brian. *George Washington's Secret Six. The Spy Ring That Saved the American Revolution*. New York: Sentinel, 2013.

Lakin, Patricia. *The Founding Fathers Were Spies! Secrets of American History: Revolutionary War*. New York: Simon Spotlight, 2017.

Lineberry, Cate. "Elizabeth Van Lew: An Unlikely Union Spy." Smithsonian.com, May 4, 2011. https://www.smithsonianmag.com/history/elizabeth-van-lew-an-unlikely-union-spy-158755584/.

National Cryptologic Museum. "Sample of Some Hobo Signs." Accessed March 15, 2019. https://www.nsa.gov/Portals/70/documents/about/cryptologic-heritage/museum/hobo-signs-definitions.pdf.

Platt, Richard. *Spy*. New York: Dorling Kindersley Publishing Inc., 1996.

Robertson, Alexander. "Revealed: How a Messenger Dog Called Satan Dodged German Fire in a Gas Mask to Help Allied Forces Turn the Tide in One of the Great War's Bloodiest Battles." DailyMail.com, February 20, 2016. https://www.dailymail.co.uk/news/article-3456252/How -messenger-dog-called-Satan-dodged-German-fire-gas-mask-help-Allied -forces-turn-tide-one-Great-War-s-bloodiest-battles.html.

Rosenberg, Aaron. *Cryptologists: Life Making and Breaking Codes*. New York: Rosen Publishing Group, 2004.

Singh, Simon. *The Code Book: The Science of Secrecy from Ancient Egypt to Quantum Cryptography*. New York: Anchor Books, 2009.

Sisk, Richard. "Vietnam-Era POW Demonstrates 'Tap Code' at POW/MIA Ceremony." Military.com, September 16, 2016. https://www.military .com/daily-news/2016/09/16/vietnam-era-pow-demonstrates-tap-code -at-pow-mia-ceremony.html.

Top Spy Secrets. "Introduction to Codes and Ciphers." Accessed February 24, 2018. https://www.topspysecrets.com/codes-and-ciphers.html.

US Navy. "US Navy Signal Flags." Official website, last updated August 17, 2009. https://www.navy.mil/navydata/nav_legacy.asp?id=273.

INDEX

··/ — ·/ — ··/ ·/ — ··—